NEURO-LINGUISTIC-PSYCHOLOGY

© Shelley Stockwell-Nicholas, PhD (310) 541-4844
Shelleynicholas@cox.net   www.hypnosisfederation.com

NLP

NeuroLinguisticPsychology

MADE EASY

Quintessential tools for happiness.

By

SHELLEY STOCKWELL-NICHOLAS , PhD

Step-by-step protocols teach YOU to.

TRAIN YOUR BRAIN using:
THOUGHT
LANGUAGE
REALITY MAPS
BODY MOVEMENT
FRAMES/ REFRAMES
ANCHORS/ TRIGGERS
PARTS INTEGRATION
STORY TELLING & METAPHOR

© Shelley Stockwell-Nicholas, PhD (310) 541-4844
Shelleynicholas@cox.net   www.hypnosisfederation.com

CREATIVITY UNLIMITED PRESS®
30819 Casilina Drive
Rancho Palos Verdes, CA. 90275
(310) 541-4844
IHF@cox.net
www.hypnosisfederation.com

© 2018 Shelley Stockwell-Nicholas, PhD

ISBN: 978-0912559-93-3
NLP (NeuroLinguisticPsychology) MADE EASY
Creativity Unlimited Press®
Library of Congress Catalog Card Number
Printed in the United States of America

Foreign rights are available. For information, or to order other books, contact: Shelley Stockwell-Nicholas, PhD; (310) 541-4844

ACKNOWLEDGEMENTS:
Thanks to Richard Neves, Michael Watson, Wil Horton, Kathi Kenedi and the many other practitioners of NLP and Hypnosis who openly share their brilliant insights and true life stories. Thanks too to the hundreds of scientists whose "evidence based" studies prove that…
YOU ARE MIRACULOUS!

NEURO-LINGUISTIC-PSYCHOLOGY

© Shelley Stockwell-Nicholas, PhD (310) 541-4844
Shelleynicholas@cox.net   www.hypnosisfederation.com

ALSO BY DR SHELLEY

ME! ARTFUL LIVING CARDS

AUTOMATIC WRITING & HEIROSCRIPTING: Tap Unlimited Creativity & Guidance

DENIAL IS NOT A RIVER IN EGYPT: Overcome Addiction, Compulsion & Fear

EVERYTHING YOU EVER WANTED TO KNOW ABOUT EVERYTHING (with McGill)

HYPNOSIS: Smile On Your Face & Money In Your Pocket

HYPNO-TAROT (with James Wanless, PhD)

INSIDES OUT: Plain Talk Poetry that talks to where you live

NLP (NeuroLinguisticPsychology) MADE EASY

THRIVE; Medical Hypnosis For Yourself and Others

MCGILL'S HYPNOTHERAPY ENCYCLOPEDIA (contributing editor)

PAIN; Stop OW Now!

SEX & OTHER TOUCHY SUBJECTS

STOCKWELL'S GREAT SHAPE HYPNOSIS– instructor's version

STOCKWELL'S HYPNOSIS DICTIONARY SCRIPT BOOK

STOCKWELL'S HYPNOSIS HISTORY, MYSTERY AND MASTERY

STOCKWELL'S STAGE HYPNOSIS MADE EASY

STORY TELLING 101 (with Peter Blum)

THE SEARCH FOR COSMIC CONSCIOUSNESS: Hypnosis Einstein Would Love (with McGill)

THE SECRETS OF HYPNOTIZING WOMEN (with Ormond McGill)

THE MYSTERIES OF MAGNIFICENT YOU

TIME TRAVEL: DO-IT-YOURSELF PAST LIFE JOURNEY HANDBOOK

WIN: COACHING GUIDE FOR YOURSELF AND OTHERS

© Shelley Stockwell-Nicholas, PhD (310) 541-4844
Shelleynicholas@cox.net   www.hypnosisfederation.com

IMAGINE:

YOU: Being your best

YOU: Healthy, wealthy and wise.

YOU: In-joying and out-joying the NOW

YOU: Helping others any time & for any reason

YOU IMAGINED THE POWER OF NLP!

NEURO-LINGUISTIC-PSYCHOLOGY

© Shelley Stockwell-Nicholas, PhD (310) 541-4844
Shelleynicholas@cox.net   www.hypnosisfederation.com

Dear YOU,

This nifty book takes the mystery out of mastery.

It helps you live the life YOU love and gives you a terrific foundation to help others do the same! As you experience each technique, you learn more about magnificent YOU and how to be your best.

Feel free to call me with your ideas and input.
Love,
Shelley Stockwell-Nicholas, PhD
YOUR NLP Coach and Trainer,
(310) 541-4844
shelleynicholas@cox.net

NEURO-LINGUISTIC-PSYCHOLOGY

NEURO-LINGUISTIC-PSYCHOLOGY

© Shelley Stockwell-Nicholas, PhD (310) 541-4844
Shelleynicholas@cox.net   www.hypnosisfederation.com

TABLE OF CONTENT

	PAGE
WHAT IS NLP?	**9**
THE NEUROLOGY OF FEELINGS	**13**
LANGUAGE THAT LINGERS	**17**
REALITY MAPS	**29**
REFLECT ON MIRRORING	**31**
FRAMES & REFRAMES	**35**
ANCHORS & TRIGGERS	**41**
SUB-MODALITY INTEGRATION	**51**
STORY TELLING & METAPHORS	**63**
NLP TAKEN FROM OTHERS	**77**
YOUR NLP CERTIFICATION	**91**

© Shelley Stockwell-Nicholas, PhD (310) 541-4844
Shelleynicholas@cox.net   www.hypnosisfederation.com

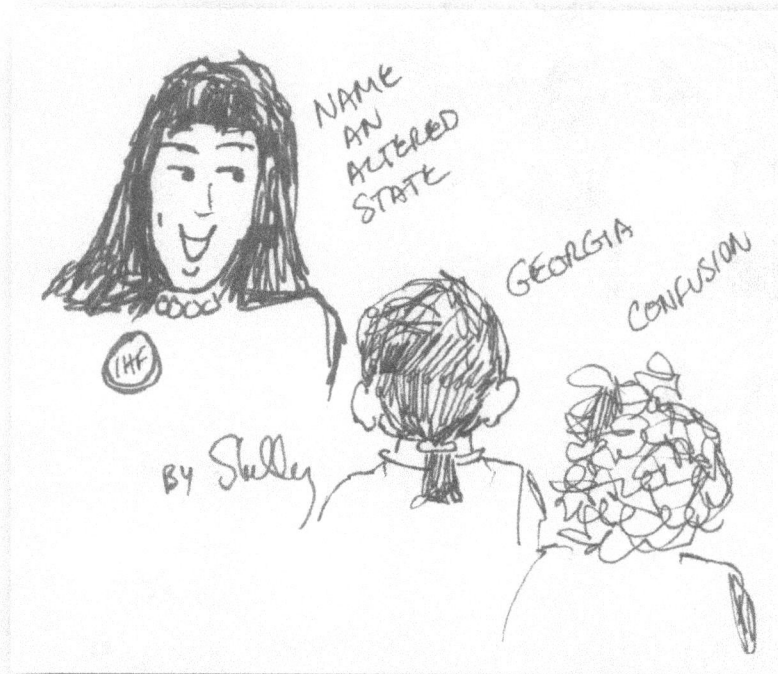

Q: *Why did Waldo (Wally) go to an NLP practitioner?*
A: *To find himself!*

© Shelley Stockwell-Nicholas, PhD (310) 541-4844
Shelleynicholas@cox.net   www.hypnosisfederation.com

WHAT IS NLP?

NLP is a set of tools and techniques used for personal motivation and leadership developement. An amalgam and descendant of hypnosis, self-actualization and humanistic psychology, NLP is heavily seasoned by protocols from the human potential movement of Jung, Erickson, Bateson, Chomsky, Satir and Perls.

"Neuro" refers to your brain cells and thoughts.

"Linguistic" relates to your use of verbal and non-verbal "language."

"Psychology" or "Programming" relates to how thoughts and communication effect your behavior. When well done, you're empowered to take charge of your thoughts, self-talk, other talk and behavior.

The main purpose of NLP is to install positive, proactive thought and action and bypass limiting thought and action. It's a terrific boon for those who want better relationships at home and work.

The National Institute of Health defines Neurolinguistic Programming as "an applied science built on linguistics, psychology and neurophysiology… Modeling and shifting these styles influences behavior for change." This same definition could be given to various hypnosis techniques as well as NLP as both influence your thought and action the same way.

THE HYPNOSIS OF NLP. Both NLP and hypnosis work their magic by engaging your imagination and flexibility. However, NLP tends to use more covert indirect approaches to induce trance. NLP also relishes it's own vocabulary.

HYPNOSIS TERMS	NLP TERMS
Suggestion and affirmation	Imbedded or installed command
Dominant senses, sub-personality, or ego state	Modalities, sub-modality, internal representation
Regress, progress, reframe	Timeline
Post-hypnotic suggestion	Future pace
Imprint	Program
Global Perception	Meta-Model

THE UP SIDE OF NLP. NLP techniques call attention to what and how you and others communicate and percieve. You more objectively identify what it's like to be "them" and more fully understand the unique world you and they create. NLP adjusts patterns of behavior!

In general, NLP explores values, mission and beliefs and helps answer questions like; "What do I need to be happy?" "How do I experience things?" "Why did I do that?" and "What needs to be done?"

THE DOWNSIDE OF NLP. Some diehard aficionados spend way too much time analyzing and/or boring a client with contrived indirect inductions (backdoor hypnosis) instead of direct inductions and getting down to the business at hand (front door hypnosis).

VAGUE MANIPULATION

By SHELLEY STOCKWELL-NICHOLAS, PhD

When I met-a-four I counted his leg

(NLPers says "it's good to be vague.")

I divided the leg by blades of grass;

their unconscious reactions saved my ass.

I chunked images, felt your toes. Heard the hair grow in your nose.

My doubletalk words swayed every thought.

(It costs me $6000 to be taught…

that you create an altered state

when you confuse and obfuscate.)

QUICK NLP LESSON

1931: NL NAME DAY. Korzybski coined the term "neuro-linguistic" and the idea that the word is not the thing itself– "The map is not the territiory" and "Language is self-reflctive."

1970: NLP NAME DAY. John Grinder and Richard Bandler added "programming."

1975: After taking a class from Grinder and Bandler, motivational speaker, Tony Robbins, claimed NLP as the foundation for his success and marketed it in books and audiotapes.

1978: PROMOTED. Robert Dilts wrote a book on NLP.

1986-1988: MURDER! Bandler, arrested for murder, was jail 120 days. A Grand Jury dropped the charges.

1996 LAW SUITS! Bandler filed a $90-million lawsuit against John Grinder, Carmen Bostic St. Clair, Christina Hall, Steve and Connirae Andreas, Lara Ewing and 200 "John and Jane Does" claiming ownership. All claims were denied. The term NLP was and, is now, labeled "public domain."

1990s: NLPt NAME DAY. Europe tagged it "NLPt" for "Neuro-Linguistic Psychotherapy."

2000: FRAUD! After Bandler's trial, Christina Hall (who held the "Society of NLP" trademark) won a $600,000 judgment over Bandler but he moved to Ireland! Then, in the UK, Bandler was convicted of receiving the NLP trademark by fraud and fined 175,000 pounds.

© Shelley Stockwell-Nicholas, PhD (310) 541-4844
Shelleynicholas@cox.net   www.hypnosisfederation.com

NAC NAME DAY: Tony Robbins, (also sued by Bandler) renamed it NAC for "Neural Associative Conditioning."

NS NAME DAYS: L. Michael Hall and Bob Bodenhamer re-named it "Neuro-Semantics."

NOW: The International Hypnosis Federation calls NLP "neurolingistics" and "Neurolinquistic Psychology."

Michael Watson calls it "Neo-Ericksonian Hypnosis."

Whatever YOU call it, it's a terrific to include powerful procedures into your tool kit and become a RELATIONSHIP and COMMUNICATION EXPERT!

© Shelley Stockwell-Nicholas, PhD (310) 541-4844
Shelleynicholas@cox.net   www.hypnosisfederation.com

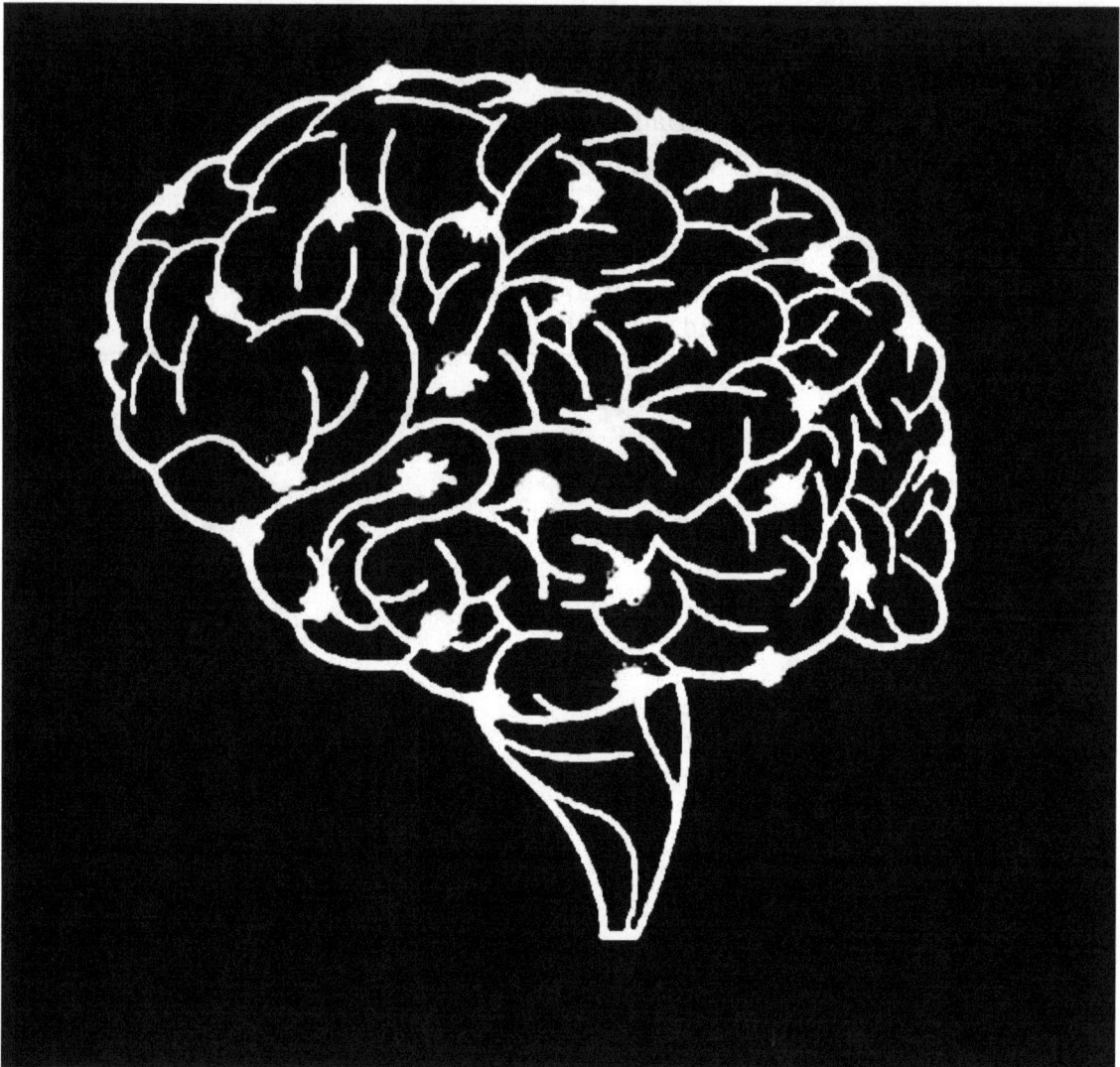

A neuron walks into a bar
The bartender says, "you can't come in."
The neuron says, "but my friends are here."
"In that case, okay" says the bartender…
The moral–or nucleus– of the story…
It's good to have connections.

© Shelley Stockwell-Nicholas, PhD (310) 541-4844
Shelleynicholas@cox.net   www.hypnosisfederation.com

THE NEUROLOGY OF FEELINGS

Ever wonder what makes you think, say and do what you think, say and do? Since NLP ostensibly employs neurology and linguistices, let's briefly explore the "neuro" part.

Someone pats you on the back and you feel a rush of pride.

You need speak and break into a cold sweat.

Someone you find attractive wafts by and you flush with excitement.

You hear beautiful music and drift away in ecstatic rhapsody.

You stop to think and forget to start again.

HOW DOES THIS HAPPEN?

Sensory receptors take and give "in-formation" that determines how you feel, act and react. then how you feel, act and react determines the structure and function of your receptors. How your senses take and give "in-formation" also determines what remains conscious or is tucked away so you don't notice it. So, what part of you recognizes, processes, remembers, learns and creates your behavior?

It's your biological self! Your biochemistry decides what you consciously notice and what remains unconscious. To a hypnotherapist the conclusion is clear: your body IS your mind! How this happens is what this article is about.

YOUR AMAZING BRAIN

You were born instinctively knowing how to lift your head, roll over or walk. It's hard-wired into your thoughts and neurology. So is your ability to speak. Your ear canals filled with sound amplifing amniotic fluid so finely tuned that, from birth to four months, you could distinguish over 150 sounds that make up human speech.

These miracles came with you as pre-programmed behavioral instructions. As you evolved and grew, you learned and honed additional behaviors that dramatically sculpted your molecules, neurons and structural development. Each biological adjustment in turn affected who you are and what you feel, think, say and do.

Your awesome brain is primarily made of water, fat and protein. No two brains are the same, and your brain is not the same moment to moment. Your brain hemispheres differ in size, gray and white matter, chemistry and structure. The very structure of your brain is influenced by how you use it.

Everything you create begins as a conscious or subconscious thought manifested in your neurology. Every instant, your brain electrochemical alters neurons and their countless links. Puberty, pregnancy, aging, past events and memory cause structure/function brain changes. Your internal and external environment sends a message to your cells. The cells receptors and their ligands then modify according to the information received and every modification affects your emotions and physiology. A cell and its modifications influence other cells.

THE MIND/BODY LOVE CONNECTION

Ever notice how your heart beats rapidly and your breathing changes when you are excited, angry or in love? Have you observed how thoughts turn you on or off sexually? Consider now how depression makes you feel physically rotten, super sensitive or numb and how happiness makes you feel free, easy and more vital.

Emotion is "e-motion" or "energy in motion." Each emotion, whether conscious or subconscious, results from an intricate biochemical action inside you that then inspires the next thing you feel. What you think emanates from your personal bio-computer. YOU AT IT. The buck stops here with YOU. YOU choose what you do. In other words, what you do and how you feel is biologically or energetically based upon decisions you make on all levels. To master this notion is what we call "free will."

HOW YOU PERCIEVE

What you see, hear, smell, taste, feel and intuit is received within a millisecond to be interpreted for meaning. How your neurology perceives what your senses receive determines if you enhance or distort it and how you place it in your memory. All input is colored by previously stored knowledge, wisdom, biases, experience, what you just ate or drank and what your were thinking. This, in turn, affects your decisions, feelings and imagination and colors what next you see, hear, smell, taste, feel, intuit and say and do.

Physical environment affects your energy. Breathing stale air in a poorly ventilated room can make you feel mentally sluggish. Physical indigestion can cause mental depression. Conversely, depression can cause illness and illness can cause depression. Arthritis-like symptoms, digestive problems, (gastric ulcers, irritable bowel syndrome, colitis, constipation, diarrhea, sinus problems) headaches (migraines) difficult breathing (upper respiratory infections asthma), heart palpitations, dizziness, arthritis, fibromyalgia, shingles and chronic fatigue result from, contribute to and activate depressing changes in brain chemistry. "The first symptoms of poor blood circulation" says Dr. H.A. Parkyn "appear in your head."

© Shelley Stockwell-Nicholas, PhD (310) 541-4844
Shelleynicholas@cox.net   www.hypnosisfederation.com

Poor memory, the inability to concentrate, sleeplessness, nervousness and headaches result and then your mental computer further reduces circulation.

WISDOM WEIGHS HEAVY ON THE MIND

The average brain weighs approximately three pounds or 51 ounces. You can figure out the weight of your brain by multiplying your weight by .01. Most lose about 4% of brain weight per decade. However, the smarter you are, the more elaborate the network between cells and the more your brain weighs. In a University of California study of 11 gifted peoples' brains, Albert Einstein had four times more oligodendroglia (glial or brain cells) than any other and some "childlike" smoothness not usually seen in adults! The visual cortex in the brain of someone with a photographic mind is twice the thickness of a "regular" brain.

HYPNOTIC SPINAL TAP EXERCISE

Think of your spinal cord as a skinny continuation of the brain in your head. Don't you love it when a chill or thrill goes up your spine? Millions (or perhaps billions) of receptors and neuropeptides in the rows of nerve ganglia line your spinal cord and instantly receive and return your brain messages. 1. Physical: Stand up and gently tap another's spine up and down and down and up.

2. Mental: **"Stand up, close your eyes and <u>imagine</u> someone is gently tapping your spine up and down and down and up. What that is like for you."** (Pause to give time to process this thought).

3. Explain: **"Focusing on a receptive nodal point activates your body's intricate neural network influencing all parts of self.You used the power of suggestion to activate receptors and ligands that make you healthy, happy and full of pep. A powerful mind/body suggestion changes you emotionally, and can stop discomfort and heal ailments."**

© Shelley Stockwell-Nicholas, PhD (310) 541-4844
Shelleynicholas@cox.net   www.hypnosisfederation.com

Doctor: *"Madam, you're filthy, you need to shower before I examine you."*
Woman: *"That's what the last doctor said."*
Doctor: *"So why didn't you do it?"*
Woman: *"I wanted a second opinion."*

© Shelley Stockwell-Nicholas, PhD (310) 541-4844
Shelleynicholas@cox.net   www.hypnosisfederation.com

LANGUAGE THAT LINGERS

Words make a difference to what you say and think. The second part of NLP is "linguistics." This chapter focuses on what you suppose and pre-suppose and offers ways to craft effective, "clean" language.

NLP assumes tenants about how you operate. A big one is that the words you choose and use stimulate awareness. Right words for you create harmony, encourage positive action, and help you give and get the most from family, friends, helpers and co-workers. Presumptive language can bring another into a better way of thinking. It can also induce trance or the learning state. The best listening is active listening where you repeat back what is said. Also called Backtracking, Feedback, Parroting or Reflective Attentive Listening that reflects content, feelings, gestures and breathing. Can be exact feedback like, **"I hear you saying…"** For clarifying; **"So what did you mean when you said…?"** and to give feedback; **"When I heard you _____ I thought _____."**

PRE-ASSUMPTIONS or PRESUMPTIVE LANGUAGE

Here are a few leading presupposing questions that evoke trance:

"When would now be a good time to do this?"

"When is now the right time to be proactive?"

"What are you pretending not to know?"

"You're now noticing how satisfying trance is for you."

"What wouldn't happen, that you don't want to happen, if you did or didn't do something?"

"What thought do you think before you say or do something?"

"If you don't have a voice in your head raise your hand… How did you know that?"

REAL LIFE HYPNO-TALE

When a client came to quit smoking, Erickson asked, "How surprised will you be when you wake up tomorrow as a non-smoker?"

"I'll be very surprised," he said.

The session was complete. In Erickson's words "I knew it would be so because he didn't question my pre-supposition."

© Shelley Stockwell-Nicholas, PhD (310) 541-4844
Shelleynicholas@cox.net   www.hypnosisfederation.com

DO THIS and THRIVE Script! "**Pre-suppose you have every resource you need to thrive** (Be rich, be trim or whatever) **and that these resources are excited to be called upon NOW… Pre-suppose that, in this moment, these resources resolve any issue that would interfere with the result you want… Imagine that in this moment, you have exactly what you want… It is a done deal. What's that like for you?**"

NLP PRESUPPOSITIONS ABOUT YOU

1. COMMUNICATE. "Your words are your map; NOT your territory." They are indicative of things and not the thing itself. Your unique messages create where you go and what you do.

2. YOUR STYLE. "Your mind/body inter-relate and communicate your style." Your dominant senses, personal symbols and modes communicate. Observe yourself and others and meet your/their mind.

3. RESOURCE. "There are no un-resourceful people only un-resourceful states." You have all the resources you need.

4. ACTION SPEAKS LOUDEST. "Behavior eclipses words, yet behavior is not who you are."

5. LEARN. "Change your story and thought and change your result." You learn to adapt resources with the context and ecology of each situation.

6. OVERCOME. A problem is a gift to shift your thoughts. "You're not broken; you're perfect. You learn from each experience."

7. CHOICE. "You don't change behavior; you make choices." NLP makes you mindfully aware and response-able. You choose and make the best choice given your resources and awareness. In this moment, you choose to be happy or miserable, calm or hysterical, notice or not notice. You choose what you do or don't do.

8. PROFOUND WISDOM. Within you is a wise, all-knowing essence that easily communicates when asked. Doing the right thing is a full-brain consensus of full awareness that relishes each moment. Noting yourself from a mindful "meta-position" awakens you from sleepwalking, "hyper-suggestibility" and "gullibility."

PRE-SUPPOSITION REVERSAL: To change limiting belief

"**In what way does** _____ (the limiting belief) **cause more** _____ (the opposite of effect)?**" Or

"**How can the opposite of this belief be true and helpful?**"

If they say, "I don't know" ask, "**As you think about it, in what way does not knowing mean you're more suitable now to deal with this?**"

© Shelley Stockwell-Nicholas, PhD (310) 541-4844
Shelleynicholas@cox.net   www.hypnosisfederation.com

> Or if they say, "I have personal flaws." ask, **"In what way, do personal flaws, actually support your personal development more than if you had no flaws?"**

SHELLEY'S PRESUPPOSITONS FOR HELPERS

In certification classes I add these presuppositions for helpers:

1. **DEEPLY RESPECT OTHERS.** No one knows a person better than they do so honor their model or perception of the world… Trust their inner wisdom's resourcefulness to do the right thing.

2. **GET OVER YOURSELF.** Be client centered. Don't impose your will (or what you assume is best for them) upon them. If you have an idea, present it and ask their inner wisdom to evaluate it from the viewpoint of their best interests.

3. **FREE WILL BELONGS TO YOU.** You have free will to think–or stop thinking– any thought here and now and so does your client.

4. **HOLD THE MIRROR FOR REFLECTION.** Stay in positive neutrality and offer feedback in the exact words and gesture and pacing that they present to you. Help them understand that everything is a story they made up, so they find the best story for themselves.

5. **AWARENESS IS NOT NECESSARY FOR RESULTS.** Transformation and heightened awareness can happen in an instant and you may not even consciously notice it.

6. **HYPNOSIS IS A NATURAL LEARNING STATE THAT EVOKES RESULTS**

CONVERSATIONAL HYPNOSIS

Conversational NLP specifically engages and motivates. Every verbal and energetic exchange, evokes reaction. You hypnotize yourself by the way you speak and understand. Your family, others influence what you think, say and do and vice versa.

REAL LIFE HYPNO-TALE: MILTON ERICKSON, MD

Erickson's client said, "I want you to help me but I don't want to do hypnosis." "Fine… Take my help in ways that serve you best." After his session, he said; "I feel better but can't remember anything."

"You may remember or forget and you will definitely leave here knowing that you received what you came for."

His face smoothed and he went into trance again.

© Shelley Stockwell-Nicholas, PhD (310) 541-4844
Shelleynicholas@cox.net   www.hypnosisfederation.com

INDIRECT (confusion) ATTITUDE-ADJUSTMENT SCRIPT

"You now notice thoughts you're not even thinking. For example, you notice your feet and, as you do, you relax more and more. Just like the chair you're sitting upon, you make an assuption that you're secure and as you do, you know that you now easily support yourself in what you want to achieve… Nod your head if you understand…"

REAL LIFE HYPNO-TALE: FROM A HYPNOSIS PROFESSIONAL

"My client said, "Chemo and radiation haven't helped my inoperable malignancy and constant pain…. I've been praying for help." Our session included these suggestions: **"You believe in prayer… that's good. The scientific word for prayer is 'hypnosis.' Let's use an ancient prayer from the Book of Alternative Services… Take it into your being… 'Highest Power, bring the Light of God into this fine person and reverse any cancer for good. Restore them to full wellness and quickly replace any discomfort with comfort and ease. Amen. Good. Let's begin…"** Nine months later, her stunned doctor said, "Your cancer is gone."

SUGGESTIVE QUESTIONING

Suggestive questioning helps clarify and bring more information to the speaker and the observer. For example they say; "They need my decision by Monday." So you ask; "Who are they?" "What do you need to decide?" and/or "What have you decided?" Especially powerful are 'Yes' questions, "Don't You" questions and "Will You" Questions.

DO THIS! "don't/aren't you" QUESTIONS

"You understand what's happening, don't you?"

"You're a positive person, aren't you?"

"You're true to your core values, aren't you?"

"You take time to evaluate what someone tells you, don't you?"

"_____ (name), listen closely, this is great for YOU …"

"You're clever, aren't you?" "You do the right thing, don't you?" and "The serenity prayer ('God grant me the serenity to accept the things I cannot change, the courage to change the things I can and the wisdom to knoe the difference') was written for you, wasn't it?"

DO THIS! "will you" QUESTIONS FOR GOOD HEALTH

"Will you ignore or look after yourself?"

"Will you court 'dis-ease' or 'ease?'"

© Shelley Stockwell-Nicholas, PhD (310) 541-4844
Shelleynicholas@cox.net   www.hypnosisfederation.com

"Will you 'manage illness' or 'effect wellness?'"
"Will your health elicit misfortune or good fortune?"
"Will you recognize and accept attitudes that expand awareness?"
HAPPY NEW ME MISSION CONTROL QUESTIONS:
1. WHAT DO I WANT? (List what you want.)

_____, _____,

Now, choose the most important thing I want.
Under what circumstances do I want it? (context)
2. WHAT DON'T I WANT?

_____, _____

3. WHAT DO I ACTUALLY DO and is it working out well?
_____

_____, _____

4. WHAT AM I NOT DOING THAT NEEDS TO BE DONE?

_____, _____

5. EMPOWERMENT
Am I flexible enough to get what I want?
Is this something I can take charge of and control?
(Parts Alignment: I bring all my sub-personalities into agreement.)

6. ECOLOGY
When I get what I want, what will be the consequences/outcome?

_____, _____

Do these fit with what I really want?
How will I know that what I do is working?
How will I know that I've gotten what I want?
(What will you see, hear, feel, smell, taste and intuit)

IN A NUTSHELL ASK ANOTHER:
1. "WHAT DO YOU WANT?"
2. "WHAT RESOURCES DO YOU HAVE TO GET IT?"
3. "WILL YOU CALL UPON THESE NOW TO MAKE IT SO?"
4. "WHAT HAPPENS WHEN YOU DO?"

LANGUAGING

Communication, in NLP terms, reflects your thoughts. When you pay attention you notice that distortions (abstraction, deletions, and mind-reading) reflect the way you analyze, categorize and create.

NEURO-LINGUISTIC-PSYCHOLOGY

© Shelley Stockwell-Nicholas, PhD (310) 541-4844
Shelleynicholas@cox.net   www.hypnosisfederation.com

Here is a rundown of languaging and suggestive questioning responses used to bring awareness to distortions:

DISTORTIONS and CLARIFYING SUGGESTIVE QUESTIONING

MIND READING "You don't like me" or "If he doesn't pay his bills, she'll leave him." **(Response:** "How do you know this?")

LOST PERFORMER "It's bad to be inconsistent."
(Response: "According to whom?" "How do you know it's bad.")

CAUSE-EFFECT "It makes me sad."
(Response: "You choose to feel sad?")

COMPLEX EQUIVALENCE "She's shouts, she doesn't like me."
(Response: "Have you ever shouted at someone you liked?")
"Now that my secretary left. I'll be bankrupt soon!"
(Response: "So your fortune depends on your secretary's employment?")

PRESUPPOSITIONS "If they knew how I suffer, they wouldn't do that."
(Response: "How do you choose to suffer?" "How are they (re)acting?
"How do you know that they don't know?")

GENERALIZATIONS/ UNIVERSALS "She (all, everyone) never (always) ignores to me." **(Response:** "Never?" "What would happen if she (all everyone) didn't ignore you?")

PERCEIVED NECESSITY OR NOT: (Should, shouldn't, must, have to, need to) "I have to take care of her."**(Response:** "What would happen if you didn't?" "Or?")
"I can't (Can't, won't) tell them the truth."
(Response: "What prevents you?" "What would happen if you did?")

NONSPECIFICS and GENERALIZING "They (everyone) rejects me."
(Response: "How, specifically?")
"There is no communication."
(Response: "Communication for what and to whom?" "How do you like to communicate?"

SIMPLE DELETIONS; Omitting important elements."They don't listen."
(Response: "Who, specifically, doesn't listen to you?")
"To do it feels bad."
(Response: "Do what exactly?")

COMPARATIVE DELETIONS:
"She's a better person." (best, worst, more, less, most, least)
(Response: "Better then whom and about what?")

PRE-SUPPOSITION: "I don't want to do it again" (they did it already)

© Shelley Stockwell-Nicholas, PhD (310) 541-4844
Shelleynicholas@cox.net   www.hypnosisfederation.com

"My wife is pregnant- or not-" (they have a wife.)
MODES OF OPERATION: Necessary: (have to, must, should) or
Possibly: (might, may) Unspecified Verbs
Global ideas (all, every, general) "Alcohol makes you say stupid things."
(Response: "What kind of stupid things?"
Specific ideas; **(Response:** Ask for bigger picture)

PAST...	=	NOW AND THE FUTURE
Hurtful Regression		Change the trigger NOW
Abandonment...		Stand On My Own Two Feet
Crisis...		Opportunity
Disempowered...		Owning Personal Power
Neglected...		Self-Nurturing
Rejected...		Self-Accepting
Pain...		Sensation, Pleasure
Lost...		Exploring

NITTY-GRITTY META-MODEL COMMUNICATION EXERCISE
A few purposeful words are effective doorways for positive change.
Do this for yourself and with a client:
1. THINK OF THE FIRST THING YOU PLAN TO SAY (Then rather than saying it, write it down.) _____ .

2. FIND ALL PRESUPPOSITIONS. How will this sentence shift the other person's experience? _____, _____

3. REWRITE YOUR SENTENCE along with the better presuppositions and say that aloud _____, _____, _____ .

4. OTHER RESPONDS. Write down the sentence again, listing all presuppositions._____,_____

IMBEDDED LANGUAGE

"Is God an atheist or does she believe in herself?" –Dr Shelley

   Imbedded commands or suggestions are words and sentence fragments intended to impact you without your being consciously aware that a suggestion was made.

   To be most effective, "mark" the suggestion by doing something different while you say it. You might lower or raise your voice pitch or

© Shelley Stockwell-Nicholas, PhD (310) 541-4844
Shelleynicholas@cox.net   www.hypnosisfederation.com

volume, tilt your head, look directly into their eyes, point to them, smile or touch the person you are talking to when you speak these ideas.

1. TRUISM OR IMBEDDED TRUISM

"You are here to learn."

"You hear my voice, and any sounds in the room. You're aware of your surroundings and the position of your arms and legs. You feel the texture of your clothes. You notice how you relax more with each easy breath. Relaxing more than a moment ago."

2. IMBEDDED QUOTES

"The best way to get even is to forget."

"Some marriages are made in heaven but they ALL have to be maintained on earth."

"Standing in the middle of the road is dangerous. You get knocked down by traffic from both ways."

"You can make a mountain out of a molehill by adding a little dirt."

"The mighty oak was once a little nut that held its ground."

"Words are the windows to the heart."

"It's all right to sit on the pity pot now and then; just be sure to flush when you are done."

3. IMBEDDED COMMANDS

"Maybe you will _____." ("…find new ways to have fun.")

"Maybe you haven't _____ yet." ("…decided to enjoy eating fresh vegetables yet."

"How would feel if you ___ ("…stopped eating chocolate cake?")"

"I wouldn't tell you to ___ ("stop eating chocolate cake") because"

"When you _____, then you _____." ("When you forgive yourself then you feel happy.")

"I was wondering _____." ("…what it would be like for you to not eat the cake tonight.")

"You probably already know _____." ("…many ways to let the weight go.")

"Don't _____ too quickly." (…go into trance too quickly.")

"Can you imagine _____?" ("…yourself 40 pounds slimmer?")

"You might notice how _____." ("…much more you relax with this next breath.")

"One (a person or people) **could/might _____ if they wanted."** ("…permanently change their eating patterns because they are having so much fun.")

© Shelley Stockwell-Nicholas, PhD (310) 541-4844
Shelleynicholas@cox.net   www.hypnosisfederation.com

"I don't know if _____" ("...you will raise your left or your right hand first.")

"You might notice how good_____ feels, when you _____."

"You may not know if _____. ("...you are going to enjoy weighing 130 pounds and then you'll find you are delighted and giggling all the time.")

"It's easy to _____, isn't it?" ("...relax")

"You are able to _____. ("...relax completely with the next thought you have.")

"...told me, _____. ("Henry Ford said/told me 'If you think you can or you can't, you're correct.'")

"A person may _____, when _____." (... remember all the good reasons donuts make them sick when they have an urge to eat one.")

"Eventually _____. (...it will be second nature to only eat fresh vegetables.)

"I could tell you that _____ but _____." ("...you are self-assured in your new slim body but I wouldn't do that")

AFFECT BRIDGE (also called Somatic Bridge, Memory Chain. Past Anchor; used to link situations, time, emotion and to connect with parts)

Note what is going on in this moment... **"What are your tears trying to say?" "What is your bouncing leg wanting to do to relax?"** or **"There is a feeling you get when you _____** (e.g. go out of control eating). **That feeling is growing very strong within you. Go back to the very first time you had that feeling...** (Or "go back to the source of that feeling)" You then use the feeling or emotion to let the person understand any re-creational connection so they let it go. Let's say they say, *"Chenille makes me feel crawly"* instruct, **"Close your eyes and think of the _____** (crawly feeling of chenille.) **Where in your body do you feel it? Good. Now a sound, word or phrase to represent that feeling** (let's say 'yuck'). **Good. Now go back in time to the first time you had _____** ('yuck' or whatever they said) **And be there 100% and tell me the first thing that comes to mind. Be there 100%.** (If necessary, prompt with questions like: **Are you inside or out? Alone or with someone? What happens next? Tell me about it. How old are you? What is going on...")** Then follow up by rising above, re-parenting and empowering your inner child, or sending off negative sub-selves or whatever else emerges from the process. Then reinforce the positive outcome and underscore the results they came to achieve.

© Shelley Stockwell-Nicholas, PhD (310) 541-4844
Shelleynicholas@cox.net   www.hypnosisfederation.com

WORD-SMITHING FOR SALES

"Benign: What comes after be-eight!"

A "business consultant" specializes in "service" (not sales.)

Your client "invests" (not pays) in top-of-the-line "quality" services (never expensive).

A contract is "the paperwork" and you "okay the agreement" along with a "form of payment" (credit card or cash) and your "fees and charges" are really commissions, additional expenses and service charges.

You may offer a "right of rescission" (meaning they can cancel) if there is "an area of concern" (an objection).

EMBEDDED WORDS TO SELL

"On the other hand… you have different fingers."

Landmark Forum seminars cleverly create "enrollment crossovers" to up-sell more seminars. The word "register" is imbedded first "so ideas *register* in your subconscious mind." Later, you're invited to "register for the program" and, finally, you "register and enroll others in future Landmark classes."

1. **Enroll Yourself** "What do you want for yourself? You need to set your intention."

2. **Enroll Support** "Tell others your plan so they share your enthusiasm. Tell them how they can assist you in getting what you want for yourself… You need to enroll others to assist you in your purpose and plan."

4. **Enroll In The Program** The word "enroll" is then used to sign up and pay for the upcoming seminars that go for about $500 for a two day class.

5. **Enroll Others to Join too.**

NEURO-LINGUISTIC-PSYCHOLOGY

© Shelley Stockwell-Nicholas, PhD (310) 541-4844
Shelleynicholas@cox.net   www.hypnosisfederation.com

One Track Mind

"Your brain is an evolutionary marvel. It starts working when you're in utero and stops when you have to figure out how to use a new computer program."
–Greg Tamblyn

© Shelley Stockwell-Nicholas, PhD (310) 541-4844
Shelleynicholas@cox.net   www.hypnosisfederation.com

REALITY MAPS

Your map of reality includes territories that may or may not support yourself to be happy, healthy and wise. As you zero in on your internal map, you meet self-talk, mindsets, and beliefs and may choose to update your perspective.

DO THIS! MODEL A WINNER

Think of someone you admire and would like to be like. (Choose someone who has accomplished what you want to accomplish.) Are they the way you want to be? If not, imagine them being exactly the way YOU want to be.

When this is so, become them... Be them... exactly as you would like them to be... Taking only the good characteristics, Now :

1. See them/ Be them... Black & white? In color? Bright or dim?

2. Feel their energy... Where do you feel them? What's the temperature?

3. Smell and taste them... Smells; pleasant or offensive? Strong or light? Are tastes sweet or bitter? Strong or mild?

4. Hear the words they/you use. Are sounds they hear loud or soft, or coming from a particular direction.

5. Imagine living in their way of being and absorb, absorb, absorb.

PLAN OF ACTION

1. WISH IT (head) Is it what I wish?

_____

2. WANT IT (heart) Is it what I want?

_____

3. DECIDE IT Is it something I decide to make happen?

_____

4. PLAN OF ACTION How will I get there?

_____

5. RESOURCES What is needed to make it happen?
(money, time and who will make it happen?)

_____

6. ACTION/IMPLEMENTATION What actions move me forward?

_____

7. ACCEPT RESULTS: STAY CONGRUENT

_____

© Shelley Stockwell-Nicholas, PhD (310) 541-4844
Shelleynicholas@cox.net   www.hypnosisfederation.com

HERE'S LOOKING AT YOU KID

UP & LEFT:
VISUAL MEMORY

UP & RIGHT:
VISUALIZING SOMETHING NEW,
LYING

STARING- DILATED:
TRANCE- RECALLING EITHER VISUAL MEMORY
OR NEW IMAGE

RIGHT OR LEFT:
SOUNDS- RECALLING OR IMAGINING

DOWN & RIGHT:
SENSING HOW THE BODY FEELS

DOWN & LEFT:
TALKING TO YOURSELF
LISTING TO YOURSELF

© Shelley Stockwell-Nicholas, PhD (310) 541-4844
Shelleynicholas@cox.net   www.hypnosisfederation.com

REFLECT ON MIRRORING

Researchers say that "ninety-three percent of communicate is based on something other than words."

We naturally imitate those around us. Mirroring and matching another are NLP techniques that help estabilsh rapport. Children model caregivers, students mirror their teachers, athletes model the coach, and the Beatles modeled the Maharishi. When you mimic another's behavior they become more receptive to ideas. Matching another's body, voice and language patterns, makes a deep bond. We watch and learn to "do what I do."

PACING AND LEADING RAPPORT

Imitate mannerisms. When you sit and move in the same way as another person does, they feel closer to you and are more likely to then follow your lead with new movements.

Subtly imitating and then shifting rhythms and patterns evokes a relaxed hypnotic state to more easily takes on suggestion. Managers who use "behavioral reflection" build motivational rapport. When credit card tele-marketers matched speaking patterns, phrses, energy, and tone with the person on the other end of the phone, they increased their sales 254% and dropped complaints 90%!

DO THIS FOR PERFECT RAPPORT!

1. **Pay Attention.** Notice any dynamics the person uses to be in control and then help them to claim and use the dynamic.

2. **Breathe Together.** Breathe in their rhythm, then slow down your breathing… they will follow.

3. **Begin With a Truism.** State the obvious. Any truism will do. Then add what is needed (e.g. **"As you sit in this fine and comfortable chair listening to the sound of my voice you may also notice that you are breathing…"**)

4. **Take them to Relaxation and YES. The obvious creates a "yes set" and lulls us into a state of agreement. ("Perhaps you notice how each breath relaxes you more and more…"**

© Shelley Stockwell-Nicholas, PhD (310) 541-4844
Shelleynicholas@cox.net   www.hypnosisfederation.com

EYES WATCHING

Eye movements indicate how you experience and process ideas. As you think or verbalize a concept or concern, your eyes move in varying patterns– up, down and back and forth as if you're watching the hypnotist's pocket watch or are in REM sleep.

If you "make something up" or tell a lie, your eyes generally go up and to the right.

Using eye movements as an induction works as well as eye fixation, where a person focuses straight ahead. In 1979 NLPers Steve and Connirae Andreas promoted eye movement integration (EMI) as a tool to "re-wire" emotional responses (EMI was later popularized by Danie Beauliau.)

MIRRORING. The word "mirroring" was coined by Francine Shapiro in 1987 for patterned eye movements. Imitating and shifting another's physical action (as in body movements, auditory tones, and tactile stimulation) influences "emotional" actions and reactions and abates stress.

STOCKWELL'S HYPNO-EYES TO CHANGE YOUR MIND:

PRE-TALK- "The process allows you to gather your feelings to reprocess them into happier more relaxed feelings. In a minute, I'll ask you to recall something while you focus your attention on my finger. Alright, are you ready to feel terrific?" Good, let's begin."

1. **"Think or recall a distressing thought or memory."** (Notice the eye movements. They might be a bare flicker, or held for minutes.)

2. **"Keep your head straight and let your eyes track the movements of my two fingers."** Or **"Focus on the** (negative thought, memory, belief, feeling) **while simultaneously moving your eyes back and forth as they follow my fingers across your field of vision. Notice whatever happens."** (Hold two fingers directly in front of their face and move them side to side about 20 times across their line of vision. Or move them opposite the movement.

3. **"Close your eyes and notice the new feelings, insights or memories that come to mind. Good."** (Repeat this several times until no distress remains.)

4. **"Let your mind go blank and notice a positive thought, feeling, image, memory, or sensation. Absorb these positive thought, feeling, image, memory, or sensation, as it becomes you."** (Enhance these positive sensations with feel-great affirmations.)

© Shelley Stockwell-Nicholas, PhD (310) 541-4844
Shelleynicholas@cox.net   www.hypnosisfederation.com

STOCKWELL'S HYPNO-EYES TO STOP DISCOMFORT:

Stand in front of the client so your hand will be 16-18 inches away from their face and ask; **"How strong is your discomfort on a scale of 1 to 10; with ten the strongest? Okay look at my finger tips with your eyes keeping your head still."** Slowly move your fingers side to side (in a 9 to 3 o'clock motion) so that they have to move the eyes to the far side each way. **"You are ready to give that discomfort away because you were created as perfect being with a perfect body and perfect mind free of defects"** Do this five or six times.

Then, when your hand is in the middle of their face, change to a diagonal motion (10 to 4 o'clock) five or six times. **"You are able to reduce discomfort as much as you wish any time you wish."** Then, in the middle again, change to 2 to 8 o'clock movement for five or six times. **"You are now feeling comfort and health through out your whole body, being perfect whole and complete, with feelings of comfort and health."** (continue to add positive suggestions) When in the middle again, change to a figure eight pattern making sure that the eyes are having to move to the far corners of the sockets. Do this three to four times.

Then change directions and make a figure eight in the opposite direction.

End in the middle and pull your hand straight away and then ask "How are you feeling now on a scale of 1-10? Repeat until they are at a lower level of stress and more comfortable.

© Shelley Stockwell-Nicholas, PhD (310) 541-4844
Shelleynicholas@cox.net   www.hypnosisfederation.com

"What would you like someone to say about you at your funeral?"
"They just moved!"

© Shelley Stockwell-Nicholas, PhD (310) 541-4844
Shelleynicholas@cox.net   www.hypnosisfederation.com

FRAMES & REFRAMES

(Also called Remodel, Redefine, and Restructure)

Meaning depends on your viewpoint and how you think and perceive. For example, a time-frame change your actions and reactions. If you have one hour to complete a task, you regard it differently than if you have one week to do it. Your mind and emotion literally shift the meaning you place on something according to its context and content.

An old picture looks completely different with a new frame around it and so do your beliefs. New ideas re-organize and re-interpret an experience. Hypnotherapist, Patti Scott, reframes the "hot flashes" of menopause as "power surges that burn calories."

REAL LIFE HYPNO-TALE: WEIGHT LOSS STUDY

Harvard's Judith Rodin, PhD, divided eighty-four hotel cleaning people into two groups. One group was told, "As you do your work, you're getting helpful exercise that will help you lose weight, be more relaxed and be stronger. Over the next thirty days, those who received this message released an average of two pounds, lowered their blood pressure by ten percent, and dropped fat percentage, mass index and waist to hip ratio. The other group remained the same.

DO THIS!
This exercise helps you put upset in the past where it belongs.
TIME LINE REFRAME TO RELEASE UPSET…

Time frames influence your action and reactions. If you have an hour to complete a task, you regard it differently than if you have one week to do it. Your unconscious knows where the past, present and future dwell. Your personal timeline can be linear, up, down or sideways. However you imagine your timeline is perfect. Five steps release an upsetting emotion using your time line.

1. "Wise Inner Mind please neutralize this upset by rising above it…

2. Go to just before the situation happened. How were things then?

3. Now, take me to immediately after the event.

4. Now, bring me forward to the here and now and remove any upset. Notice how terrific that is.

5. Now move into the future where I enjoy the ripple effect of the new neutrality and wonderful attitude you create within me."

DO THIS! YOUR HAPPY OUTCOME THREE STEP...

If at first you don't succeed; change your definition. But how do you reframe a deeply imbedded "frame" or imprint? Use these three easy steps...

1. **MARK YOUR ACTIONS.** First notice or "mark" the gestures, voice tone (pitch or volume) and facial expression you use when thinking or talking about a negative limit. In other words, what behaviors go along with that idea. Notice your tilt of the head, if you look someone in the eye, and your facial expression. (gestures that go along with words are sometimes called "id-entities)

2. **CHANGE YOUR ACTIONS.** Now change your gestures, voice tone and facial expression as you think or talk about the issue.

3. **CHANGE YOUR WORDS.** Your verbal spin makes all the difference in how you feel. **"What else could this mean?"** Create the best story for yourself. Pain and stress are relieved when you put a new story frame around it. Suggestions as, **"The feeling of... described as _____** (a problem) **now feels soothing like soft water flowing gently upon you,"** can do wonders.

DO THIS! HAPPY OUTCOME TO HELP OTHERS

To reframe limiting beliefs and resolve "blocks".

1. **DISCOVER with RAPPORT.** the person's goals, history, beliefs and verbal and physical expression (representational system).

2. **INTERVENTION.** Suggestive questioning is individually tailored to the person's style to instill confidence, congruency and mindful strategies for desired behavior, self-talk and results.

3. **IMPLEMENTATION LASTING RESULTS.** Timeline of the past, present and the future you want to achieve and instilling confidence and a well-formed outcome.

DR. NEVES' PHOBIA THEATER IN SEVEN STEPS

A reframe as a teaching tale has excellent impact. He says that this NLP process neutralizes upset, fear and trauma by "disconnecting anchors." When you review past, present and future from a more objective perspective you create a better story to tell yourself.

© Shelley Stockwell-Nicholas, PhD (310) 541-4844
Shelleynicholas@cox.net   www.hypnosisfederation.com

Here is how to use it and say good-bye to bugs that bug you or fear of heights, birds, snakes, water, elevators… or whatever:

Step One, INTENTION SETTING: Have your client tell you about an unpleasant memory, phobia, or trauma. As they do, notice their physical responses. If they get very emotional, have them look up and take a full breath and they will pull out of the upset state.

Step Two, COMFORT: Have them imagine themselves relaxing as they sit in a comfortable seat in a movie theatre. There's a large screen up front. Up and to the left of the screen is a silent black and white photo of themselves just <u>before</u> the upset or phobia. Up and to the right of the screen is a black and white photo of themselves <u>fully relaxed</u> and comfortable with no sound <u>after the upset is over</u>. (comfort zone to comfort zone).

Step Three, DISSOCIATED VIEW: "Imagine floating out of your body to the back of the theatre, so you're watching yourself, watching yourself on the comfortable picture of you on the left…"

Step Four, DETACH and OBSERVE UPSET: "In a moment you will flick the switch and the image or perception on the left will turn into a movie. It will stay black and white, with no sound as you watch yourself watching yourself going through the experience (fear, accident, illness…) **Do this quickly, as I count from 1 to 5 the movie will run all the way to the other side. Ready, throw the switch and go, 1-2-3-4-5. Make sure you get to the other side and relax."**

Step Five, RE-ASSOCIATE: "Jump into your body in that comfy seat then get up and walk over to the picture of yourself on the right after the upset. Step into the still picture and let it turn into full living color. As the color becomes you rapidly run the movie backwards, with sights, sounds and feelings. It is like you're inside the movie as it runs backwards. Do this very quickly, as we reverse the count from 5 to 1. 5-4-3-2-1, done! Open your eyes."

Step Six, TESTING: "Think of the event and notice your comfort level." If it's fine, you're done. If not, go back and do step five a few more times.

Step Seven, FUTURE PACE: Ask about their old fear and see their response. They will be calm and neutral.

DO THIS! NLP CPR FOR A BROKEN HEART...

Hypnotist Kate Ellis uses the NLP movie theater technique for mending a broken heart. Here's my version of her approach. It works well with folks who have a keen imagination and are visually dominant. Try it, you'll like it: **"Imagine yourself sitting in a posh chair in a movie theater. On the screen is a super big color photo of yourself. If you are not a particularly visual person, you might notice how you feel being that photo. What is around you? What are you wearing?**

Next imagine yourself in the projection room and about to show you a movie about your relationship. When both the 'you' in the theater and 'you' in the booth are ready, run a movie about the great things that happened in your romance; the fun, the passion, the gentle moments, all the sweet memories. If you get misty watching the movie, that's fine.

Now rewind that movie all the way back to before you ever met. Take it off the projector and put on the next feature: It's a movie about the bad parts of your relationship... your pet peeves, the injustices, hurts, and disappointments... It's okay to growl watching this movie.

When done, rewind that movie too and relax back into your comfy seat. How happy you are as you look up at the screen and enjoy a happy picture of yourself smiling back at you saying: "I'm glad that's over."

Finally, project a movie of yourself five years from today; happy in a new life surrounded by love. That old relationship is the past. You are now in a new moment of joy. And you say 'thank you' to that person and that relationship that didn't work out five years ago. 'You taught me so much about loving myself and making healthy choices in love. All the past is forgiven and I have matured and grown into a happy, successful and loving one.' You leave the theater and enjoy a beautiful night sky and, if you happen to see that old flame again, you feel comfortable and complete."

"As captain of a battleship, I command you; change your course or we will collide."
"Your call. I will not change my course… I'm a lighthouse…"

© Shelley Stockwell-Nicholas, PhD (310) 541-4844
Shelleynicholas@cox.net   www.hypnosisfederation.com

ANCHORS & TRIGGERS

When an association brings up a memory and/or a mind/body/emotion that triggers an internal or external response, NLPers and Hypnotists call it "anchoring." Anchoring is your innate non-verbal communication and automatic state change.

If "our song" brings a tear to your eye? Or you salivate when you smell cinnamon rolls… you're anchored.

When you associate a stimuli with a response or a mind/body/emotional state with something else, you're anchored. Anchoring as your natural, automatic biofeedback response.

Anchors and triggers happen naturally or can be set up. A natural one occurs when you touch a person, say their name, and look them in the eye. You anchor a connection and a memory peg that you can retrigger with the same touch, word or gesture.

Do you see the golden arches and want a hamburger? If so, you're anchored and triggered. Advertisers spend a fortune to anchor their product with the celebrity who hypes it.

Studies show that touch yields bigger tips for a waitress, and you buy more if you're touched by a store greeter. One NBA study concludes; the more chest bumps, high fives, and backslaps, the more successful the team and the individual.

Metaphors and stories anchor. So do anything that stimulates your senses… burning sage, incense, popcorn at the movies and odors of all sorts are olifactory anchors that can evoke a nueral response.

Like a string of pearls, you associate one thing with another.

ANCHORING IN A NUTSHELL. Anchoring is a conditioned response that you associate with something else (that is sometimes called the trigger); an alarm clock, stop light, touch, sound/word, smell, taste, sight or sequence are associated cues that evoke you to re-experience or remember a specific experience. This often includes a strong emotion. The stimuli and response are imprinted and stays with you when you repeat or recall the experience or the associated cue. This is fine if it makes you happy. It's miserable if it causes upset.

SELF-HYPNOSIS: HI OH TRIGGER AWAY.

You can establish anchors for resourceful states of relaxation, creativity and motivation. You can use anchoring to eliminate an unwanted thought or behavior.

© Shelley Stockwell-Nicholas, PhD (310) 541-4844
Shelleynicholas@cox.net   www.hypnosisfederation.com

Past glory or wounding imprints your very core. To heal past hurts, you train yourself via self-talk not to automatically react emotionally (you become neutral). You then choose what experience you heed or ignore. This is easily and rapid when you mentor yourself out of painful meanings, beliefs and thoughts and replace them with soothing meanings, beliefs, and thoughts.

POSITIVE ANCHORS

NLP and hypnosis installs knee jerk reactions that kick-in new positive responses. They anchor positive feeling for success that you can later "trigger" to bring back the great feelings. Hypnotic anchors can be a touch (grip, tap, posture, positioning), smell, sight (color, symbol, icon, brightness), action. gesture, facial expression, sound (voice, tempo, phrase, buzzword, mantra), vibration, feeling, taste, that links to elicit positive results in waking and sleeping life.

During a session your helper might gently touch your wrist when you laugh. If so, they "set" an anchor. Joy and that touch are now linked to a touch on your wrist. Later in the session they may "fire off" this anchor by touching your wrist and saying, **"You now happily accomplish your goal."**

When you hypnotize someone confidence (anchor it!).

My "Dr Shelley's Hi Ho Trigger" works wonders when I tell a client, **"Touch your thumb to your forefinger in the okay sign. Good. 'Whenever you touch your thumb and finger together like this you remember 'I am in charge of my behavior and feel terrific...' You feel terrific, just as you do right now! You simply touch your thumb to your forefinger and these wonderful feelings instantly come right back."**

In trance, a hypnotist may also suggest, **"It's safe in your world. There's a bubble of protection that surrounds you. To remind yourself, touch this place on your wrist and you'll recall afresh that this invisible protective energy completely encapsulates you."**

You can set up a naturally occuring anchor as; **"My voice will go with you. Whenever you see a flash of color** (or hear your name or smell the coffee...) **you'll immediately recall my words and act and react from these wonderful ideas."**

Hypnotic anchors link good feeling to positive results. Hypnotically adopting an idea, buzzword or phrase in your waking life evokes a conditioned stimuli/response and a post hypnotic suggestion that brings

© Shelley Stockwell-Nicholas, PhD (310) 541-4844
Shelleynicholas@cox.net   www.hypnosisfederation.com

about an intense neurological state… For example: **"Every time you see your wedding ring on your finger you say to yourself 'I enjoy getting along with my mate.'"** Or **"Every time I see the color green I say to myself I love fresh food."** Or **"Each breath is like a prayer that reminds you, it's safe in your world. There's always a surrounding bubble of protection around you. To remind yourself, simply touch the inside of your hand and an invisible protective energy will completely encapsulate you."**

A runner might say, "full speed" or "full energy" to automatically activate more push.

A weight releaser may say the name of a movie stat and feel motivated to pass up dessert to look just like their hero.

A sexual enhancer might say, "blissful and vital," to feel sexier.

A test taker says, "I open my mind to all knowledge" to activate the brain to learn and remember.

THREE FINGER RELAXATION METHOD: While in a relaxed state instruct, **"Touch the tips of your index and middle finger with your thumb. Anytime during the day you want to relax, just touch your fingers together, take a deep breath and say to yourself 'relax.' And you will instantly take it easy."**

Or **"Touch the tip of your tongue to where your teeth and upper palate meet."**

INSTANT ELMAN ANCHOR A SAFE PLACE RE-INDUCTION

"Close your eyes and think about a place you like in nature." (Touch their knuckle)…

(Now, release the touch) **"At the count of three, open your eyes… 1…2…3… Open your eyes!**

(Touch the knuckle again) **Now, close your eyes and sleep."**

ANCHOR TO RE-MEMBER:

(Dan Cleary's Idea) **"Take a deep breath... Hold it. Let go of any concerns. Touch your finger or... a toe... or just feel the way you do... for a moment... You re-member that all learning is in awareness ... You know how to re-member any learning you want to... you re-member ... easily ... now."**

© Shelley Stockwell-Nicholas, PhD (310) 541-4844
Shelleynicholas@cox.net   www.hypnosisfederation.com

STOCKWELL'S NEGATIVE ANCHOR FOR HEALTH

You can anchor in negative feelings as a form of aversion therapy. **"Any time you see toxins in any form, you think this vile, gross, disgusting thing. This vile, gross, disgusting thing is all mixed up in your head. AND if you touch your thumb to your forefinger in the okay sign, you remember that you are in control of your behavior and feel terrific."**

ANCHOR A MAGIC EMOTIONAL RESET BUTTON SCRIPT

"This simple magic reset process distracts your brain from an undesirable reaction. It stimulates and distracts your brain's emotional amygdala to take it easy. If you're off base, you'll simply touch your magic reset button, and feel and think the way you would rather think and feel. Are you ready? Great... Let's do this in three easy steps. Step 1. Choose a convenient spot on your body that you can touch in a socially acceptable manner. (e.g. your forehead between your eyes above the brow.)

Step 2. Touch the tip of your index finger on that spot, and at the same instant conjure up the feeling of being calm, at ease, and in control. This familiar, relaxed way of being is now your emotional home base. It's the place you want to come back to easily. Nod your head if you agree. Very good.

Step 3. Instuct your inner knower, higher self or internal observer to remind you to return to your peaceful zone here and NOW. Nod your head when this is so. Excellent. By touching this magic reset button you will amaze yourself by the fine results. You have full control you have over your emotions and reactions. You feel great. Soon your reset button will automatically relax you without even having to physically touch it. You are in charge and in control!"

DOES THE NAME PAVLOV RING A BELL?

Pavlov's dog was conditioned to salivate when a bell rang. The bell and the saliva response were anchored together. Pavlov called this the "law of association." In this same way, anchors positive feeling with a stimuli...

ANCHORING KEYS

According to Pavlov, a well-formed anchored stimuli or conditioned reflex can last a lifetime. Will Horton underscores four ways to successfully install a long lasting anchor:

© Shelley Stockwell-Nicholas, PhD (310) 541-4844
Shelleynicholas@cox.net   www.hypnosisfederation.com

1) **Intensity:** The stronger the senses the more resourceful it will be. Intensity increases your association.

2) **Timing;** Set an anchor at the peak of the experience. The longer you maintain intensity, the more the anchor is established

3) **Uniqueness;** Different anchors and uncommon or unique experiences make bigger impressions.

4) **Repetition;** The more often you anchor good feelings, the stronger the anchor will be. Practice makes perfect in anchoring. When you build and replicate an anchor you more strongly instill it into your mind. Compounding 're-anchoring' is called 'stacking anchors.'

STOCKWELL'S PAIN RELIEF SCRIPT; ANCHOR COLLAPSE

"Close your eyes. You're about to feel terrific in every way. Which is your dominant hand? Good. Focus on your other hand. Hold it out, palm up... and pretend that any discomfort is in the palm of this hand... If this were a color, what color would it be? (Client responds)...

Good! Is the color transparent, translucent or opaque? (responds)...
Bright or dull? (responds). **Good.**
What symbol would it be? (responds).
If it had a sound what would that be? (responds).
Good.
What does it look like? (Client responds and you repeat it back).
If you suddenly release this, how wonderful you feel! So release it. Focus all your imagination now on letting it go completely as you release it once and for good. (Pause)... **What color best symbolizes this great feeling.** (responds). **Good!**
What feeling and texture is in your hand now? (Client responds as you repeat it back). **Good! What sound does it have?** (responds).
What vibration or energy? (responds and you repeat) **That's great!**
How does it look? (Client responds) **Splendid.**
Put both hands together and feel great! In your hands is a toy you can play with. Go ahead toss it or pet it and enjoy this toy. It brings happiness and you feel good. You feel great. What a fine, permanent relief! You did it! Open your eyes... Very good!

DR SHELLEY's JOYOUS ANCHORING FOR YOU

1. **"Think of something that makes you smile. Make the smile even bigger and, if you really want to be happy, laugh. That's right. Laugh out loud... You don't even have to believe it... just laugh out loud.**

© Shelley Stockwell-Nicholas, PhD (310) 541-4844
Shelleynicholas@cox.net   www.hypnosisfederation.com

Good. Injoy and out-joy this laugh through all of your senses.

2. Find the place inside yourself where you feel your joy of laughing. This is your internal happy place and you are now send feel great endorphins through your entire body and mind.

3. Now, associate people, activities and your very being with how you feel in this moment...

Give this experience a color. Just the thought of the this color makes you smile and chortle.

Now give yourself a cue (touch a knuckle or the inside of your hand or touch your thumb to your forefinger in the okay sign) **and decide that if ever you need an attitude adjustment. you will trigger your joy response in this way.**

4. Great job! Okay laugh again and as you do try to find a miserable thought... It's not going to happen... Joy is now your compass.

CONFLICTING ANCHORING TO SOLVE ISSUES

Pavlov also noted that when a negative and positive anchors were used at the same time a dog would not respond to either but became "passive." It is the same with us, seemingly confusing contradictory feelings evoke neutrality. Mental confusion ("cognitive dissonance") can be used for an induction and to solve problems. NLPers call upon conflicting achors to evoke an anchor collapse.

DR SHELLEY'S ANCHOR COLLAPSE PROTOCOL:

1. **BRING UP A NEGATIVE MIND STATE: "Recall a difficult situation**...(e.g upset or troubling thought). As they do, gently squeeze their right shoulder and say **"I know it was upsetting."** Then remove your hand. (Optional; have them open their eyes and do small talk- This is called a "separator state")

2. **BRING UP A POSITIVE STATE: "Remember a time when things were good and positively exciting?"** As they recall this, gently squeeze their left shoulder. You can test the positive results by squeezing the shoulder again and saying, "That feels better than the other one, right?" Release. **"So if you are ready to feel fine in every way smile? Great!"**

3. **BRING UP BOTH STATES and NEUTRALIZE**: Squeeze both shoulders (or "triggers") at the same time saying, **"Confusion is learning. Close your eyes, take a fine breath and it all clears up. Both shoulders are comfortable and relax."** Or **"You now allow your mind to make a better choices"** (Release both your hands and be still.)

© Shelley Stockwell-Nicholas, PhD (310) 541-4844
Shelleynicholas@cox.net   www.hypnosisfederation.com

4. AFFIRM THE RESULT.

(After several minutes ask;) **"What is going on?"** Then squeeze the negative right side to assure that there is no longer a negative reaction. The old anchor will be gone and they'll feel fine. Ask, **"How are you now regarding ———** (the original issue...) When it is gone, have them open their eyes.)

Or say **"If you try to think about what was bothering you, and can't even bring it back!")** (You can also say, **"It's now neutral"** as you touch both shoulders again.)

ANCHOR NEW PARENTING PROGRAMS

1. Think of a Parent Problem. **"Close your eyes and think of time in the past when your parent** (or parents) **made a choice that affected you negatively."**

2. Anchor the Icky (problem state). **"When that unhappy thought comes to mind, touch your left shoulder with your left hand."** (or you the hypnotist, touch their shoulder or hand).

3. Think of A Gift You Hold (resource state) **"Think of fine qualities that you have now that you wish your parents had then; qualities like bravery, compassion, thoughtfulness, practicality, and/or a sense of humor.... Good."**

4. Anchor Strength. **"When that happy thought of your fine qualities comes to mind, touch your right shoulder with your right hand."** (Or you, the hypnotist, can touch their other shoulder or hand)."

5. Anchors Away. **"Keep your hand on your right shoulder** (or you, the hypnotist, remains holding the positive anchor), **Imagine your parent**(s) **having this same precious resource and notice how it would affect the choices they made in that time long ago. Now also put your left hand on your left shoulder** (or, you the hypnotist use both the negative and positive anchor at the same time). **You now freely relive that old memory in a new way. When you are complete smile, drop your hands in your lap** (or hypnotist stops touching the anchor) **and open your eyes."**

6. Check In. **"As you think about the past, what difference do you notice?"**

CHAINED ANCHOR COLLAPSE

Michael Watson teaches your to establish then tap four anchors (from shoulder to hand) in a row to release an unwanted behvior.

© Shelley Stockwell-Nicholas, PhD (310) 541-4844
Shelleynicholas@cox.net   www.hypnosisfederation.com

1) **Worst Scenerio**
2) **Typical Scenerio**
3) **Desired Response**
4) **Enhanced Desired Response**
The negative disolves and is proven when you tap the original negatives.

BANDLER's GODIVA CHOCOLATE PATTERN

This fun process was born when a woman said, "I love Godiva chocolate and I hate doing paperwork." The idea is to hold two thoughts in the mind so you're motivated to do something you've been less inspired to do. It somehow cross-wires and empowers you to do it! (In this woman's case she now associates doing paperwork as as much fun as chocolate.) In a nutshell: Two images: ONE, what you fully like and embrace (associate). TWO what your want to embrace (disassociated.) Let ONE what you like absorb TWO. Now both are associated.

DO THIS! NLP NEW BEHAVIOR INSTALLATION SCRIPT:
1. MOTIVATION THOUGHT: "Think of something you wildly enjoy doing. Notice how it makes you feel. Create a vivid idea of it in your mind. Set this aside."
2. GOAL: "Think of something you would like to feel better about or more motivated to do and you'll find you enjoy doing this even more!"
3. ALL PARTS AGREE (ECOLOGY CHECK): "Are all parts of you ready to enjoy doing and being more motivated to enjoy and do this thing?" (If not, change it's mind...) **Good! All parts of you–physical... mental... emotional... and spiritual– are eager for you to use your natural resource to make things better for you."**
4. OPENING: "Imagine the thing you so enjoy doing and put this in front of the thing you want to enjoy more. Open up a hole in the thing you enjoy that is big enough to see the thing you would like to enjoy more peeking through it. (It can open like the iris of an eye) The good feeling of doing what you so enjoy doing is now permeating the thing you are enjoying more and more. The opening permeates good feelings into what you want to do and you now feel great about it
5. KEEP FEELING GOOD: "Check it out; your goal is now saturated with good feelings and thoughts. You are drawn to it and look forward to enjoying wellness the way you really enjoy things fully ..."

LETTER TO A QUIT SMOKING CLIENT
(Thanks to Joan Broadhurst, CCHt for the idea.)
Give this letter to give your client after teaching them anchoring...

© Shelley Stockwell-Nicholas, PhD (310) 541-4844
Shelleynicholas@cox.net   www.hypnosisfederation.com

Congratulations _____ (Client's name)You've learned a wonderful and powerful self-hypnosis technique- the anchor!

Use it whenever you need to feel great!

Old toxic habits have been "reprogrammed" and are now in the past. You're now free to breathe with ease. If ever you wonder about putting any burning leaves into your perfect lungs, you immediately STOP and your anchor reminds you to breathe with ease and you naturally take a full breath of fresh air and then do something else. Your new Breath anchor keeps you calm and relaxed. If ever you think a stressful idea, you automatically return to peace and engage your powerful anchor by taking a nice full easy breath. The more frequently you use this technique, the easier and quicker it is for you to be calm and relaxed.

For the next thirty days you will drink six to eight glasses of water daily and eat healthy nutritious foods. You'll find that you are interested in natural nutritious foods and are satisfied to eat for fuel and you stop eating when you are fueled.

Your decision to be healthy is strong within you and this technique makes this easy for you. Welcome to good health.

Congratulations! YOU BREATHE WITH EASE.

Your Hypnotist, _____ (your name)

© Shelley Stockwell-Nicholas, PhD (310) 541-4844
Shelleynicholas@cox.net   www.hypnosisfederation.com

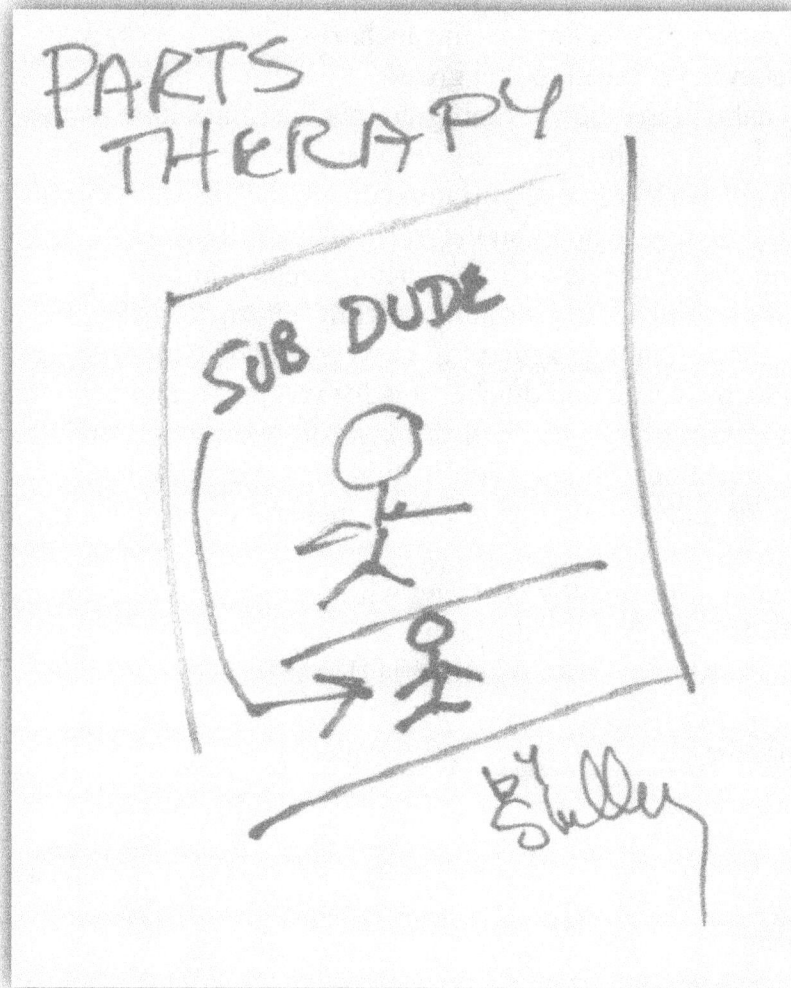

Client: *"I snore so loudly, I keep myself awake."*
Coach: *"Sleep in another room!"*

© Shelley Stockwell-Nicholas, PhD (310) 541-4844
Shelleynicholas@cox.net   www.hypnosisfederation.com

SUB-MODALITY INTEGRATION

(PARTS THERAPY)

You're a many spendored thing. Various modes of perception uniquely process data via your "dominant senses." Any trance or "sub-modality" may itself be a sub-personality. Parts perception is a "representational system" that makes you whole and holy. That's what this chapter is about.

"Why is it when you talk to God you're praying, but when God talks to you, you're schizophrenic?" –Lily Tomlin

Today I... no, that wasn't me…

A multitude of sub "you's," or sub-personalities, dwell within the vastness of YOU. Each serves a distinct purpose and each shows up as a teacher to enhance self-awareness.

SHADOWS OF ME

"I have a little shadow that moves in and out of me
And what can be the use of it is more than I can see
It is very, very like me from my feet up to my head
And I see it jump before me when I jump into my bed."

GOALS OF SUB-PERSONALITY WORK

"A part of me loves all the viewpoints and opinions of my personalities!" –Shelley Stockwell-Nicholas, PhD

Integration. Sub-personality work coaches help you to be at one with duality. It aligns thought, feelings, archetypes, ego states, identities, inner family, organs, past-present-future self, and mind-body-spirit. Carl Jung said, "Fragmentary personalities can live their own life apart from your intentions" so one goal of parts work is to explore and harness all viewpoints, thoughts and opinions so they fly in formation. Your most dominant and helpful sub-personality becomes your "Master Coach" who enlists and cheers on other inner voices to reach goals.

Eliminate Conflict. Four people lived in one head. Their names were Everybody, Somebody, Anybody, and Nobody. When an important job was needed to be done, Everybody was sure Somebody would do it. Anybody could have done it, yet Nobody did it. Somebody was annoyed and said, "This is Everybody's job." Everybody said, "Anybody could do it. But when Nobody realized Everybody wouldn't do it, Everybody blamed Somebody when Nobody did what Anybody could do."

Creativity. Neal Gabler recalls; "Walt Disney would enter trance and uninhibitedly transform himself into Mickey or Donald or an owl or an old hunting dog... He would imitate the expressions of the dog, and look from one side to the other, and raise first one brow and then the other, so animators would know what to draw." Disney also personified three "personas" in business... "The Visionary" who focused on what was wanted, "The Realist" who focused on how to get there and "The Nay-Sayer" who pointed out potential pitfalls.

Health and Fun. Parts put a positive spin on the past, reduce stress and conflict, improves luck, ups your immune response, and evokes fun. Most processes begin with a statement of purpose from each inner/outer voice. This familiarizes you with your wisdom and foibles so you underscore good judgment and eliminate or reframe limiting messages.

Trance Induction. Your many voices can evoke an easy slide into altered states with no formal induction.

Balanced and Centered. When you teach seeming opposed sub-selves to respect each other's purpose and get along, you center yourself in a dynamic and shifting harmonious flow of here and now. A Buddhist proverb says, "To know your past... Look to your present. To know your future... Look to your present." This makes making a living now your fluid wave of the future.

THE SUB-PERSONALITIES OF SUB-PERSONALITIES

"I have opinions of my own- strong opinions- but I don't always agree with them." –George Bush, US President

NLP calls upon the fine work of Virginia Satir, Fritz and Laura Perls and others encouraged dialoguing with your many inner voices and viewpoints so you embrace and personify distinct mini-selves or inner/outer voices. Tribal people dress, dance and speak from various parts of their being. Indigenous ones may embody totems. Religions categorize deities to represent sub-self embodiments like angels and devils. We still use ancient Egyptian astrological signs to represent characteristics and attitudes. In recent times many variations of this multiplicity theme are sold under sub-personality sub-names.

Whatever you call it– from channeled voices to scientific pontification– as you get in touch with your sub-selves you become more whole and complete.

© Shelley Stockwell-Nicholas, PhD (310) 541-4844
Shelleynicholas@cox.net   www.hypnosisfederation.com

SUB-PERSONALITIES: A ROSE BY MANY NAMES	
1935. Archetypes (Carl Jung) **1940. Gestalt** (Fritz & Laura Perls)	**Polypsychism** (magnetizer Durand or DeGrof)
1953. Ego Feelings or Ego States (Paul Federn, John G. Wilkins)	**Psycho-Imagination** (Joseph Shorr) **Psycho-Synthesis** (Roberto Assagioli)
Engram Therapy **Ecology,**	**Selves Inside You** (Stewart Shapiro) **Inner Child Work** (Eric Berne)
Disassociation (Pierre Janet) **Imagineering** (Walt Disney)	**Hypno-Analysis & Sub-Personality** (Shelley Stockwell-Nicholas)
Family Constellations (Bert Hellinger) **Fugue or Disassociation**	**1989. Voice Dialogue** (Hal and Sidra Winkleman-Stone)
Holodynamics (Vernon Woolf) **Transactional-Analysis** (Eric Berne)	**Parts Therapy** (popularized by Virginia Satir then Charles Tebbits.)
Psychodrama (Alfred Adler)	**Modality Integration**
Integration, Mini-me's, Past life	**Sub-Modalities Therapy**"

CENTER INNER VOICES FOR GREAT RELATIONSHIPS

My wonderful brother, Sasha Lessin, PhD, writes: "If you unconsciously project a negative sub-personality, you sour relationships. YOU get along with others by getting along with your sub-selves. Invite any hurt, fear or angry sub-self to express themselves and from a centered awareness integrate them with love. The selves you think you are and ones you show others can make or break a relationship. The keys to this;

1. **EXPRESS.** Express hidden inner voices. Let them share hurts, insecurities and communicate even that traits you hate.

2. **REVIEW PAST PARTS ORIGINS.** How did you develop your inner selves? As a little kid you needed parental love to live, get along and feel okay, so you imprint certain behavior from younger times. If you were needy then, your Inner Child, may be expressed as a needy sub-self now.

At five, my Inner Critic won my Dad's approbation. I was jealous when Mom nursed my baby sister, as I'd been bottle-fed. Mom covered her breast and said, "Shelley's a girl, I can cuddle her because she's just going to marry someone and doesn't need to study like you. Now go study your verb wheel."

I hated baby Shelley. When I thought nobody saw, I sneaked into her room and twisted her foot. She cried. Dad said, "Don't hurt your little sister. Make nice to her. Pet her like you pet your kitty." Later, when no one guarded the baby I again went to hurt her. I replayed Dad's command, "Don't hurt the baby" and this inner voice, my Inner Critic, stopped me. If

© Shelley Stockwell-Nicholas, PhD (310) 541-4844
Shelleynicholas@cox.net   www.hypnosisfederation.com

I acted out my Jealous Voice impulses, my vulnerable Inner Child would experience fear and hurt from Dad's anger.

My Critic converted an attack to a love gesture. Rather than hurt Shelley, I stroked her hair. She smiled. As our eyes met we fell in love. My parents noticed and praised my behavior. My Critic saved me from disapproval and won me praise. Thus, protective voices developed.

Your Inner Child develops protective voices to make people like you. Protective voices dictate how to get what you want. They say what to do and what to avoid so people- especially your family– won't scorn, shun, neglect, punish or abuse you.

Protective voices hide vulnerability and hurt. If parents disliked your sub-voices you may stop showing these voices. Or repress them from awareness. You project hidden, unconscious voices when you react with discomfort or envy seeing them in other people. The Child gives or retracts warmth as the grown you relates to others. It says whom you can trust. It says 'leave painful situations you can't change.'

CENTERING INNER VOICES SCRIPT

(Thanks to Hal Stone & Sidra Winkelman for some of these ideas)

MEET YOUR CENTER. "Sit here. This is the position the place from which you hear all your inner voices. Let's call it your Center '_____' (the person's name). **Good."**

MEET MAIN VOICE. "Tell me about one of the main voices you present to the world. What is the name of that voice? [For example Intellect, Critic, Pleaser, Pusher]. **What does it do for you?**

Shift your seat/cushion to a new position for that voice _____

[If a voice would like to speak but it would rather not be embodied, talk about it from your Center.]

"Hi. _____ What may I call you? [The name of that main voice]
What's your job?
When did your life start? (Or, "How long have you been around?")
What's your history with _____ (the person's actual name)?
What do you do?
What would you like to be appreciated for?
What voices do you protect?
What contributions have you made to _____ (person's actual name)?
What would you like to be acknowledged and appreciated for?
Thank you, I liked talking with you.

© Shelley Stockwell-Nicholas, PhD (310) 541-4844
Shelleynicholas@cox.net   www.hypnosisfederation.com

Let _____ (the person's actual name) **return to the Center position."**

CHECK IN WITH CENTER AND OTHERS. "Hi, Center. What did you notice that _____ **(the sub-self) embodied? Tell me about another of your voices or sub-selves…"**

(Continue with other voices e.g. Instinctual, Creative Voice, Kid, Sexy and move to a seat for each voice. Enact this as voices 2, 3 and 4 in the same way always using the name given and the questions. When complete, invite back Center.) **"Thank you, I liked talking with you. Let** _____ **(the** person's name) **return to the Center position?"**

WHAT IS LEARNED. Hi, _____ (The person's name and the Center… Wrap it up with;) **"Stand behind me and face the spaces you occupied for each voice as I summarize what you said as each.**

Feel each voice's energy as a neutral observer."

(Summarize what each sub-self said and end at the Center.)

"From this place of center what have you learned."

WIN EXERCISE; DR SHELLEY'S SUB-PERSONALITY DIALOG:

"Let me speak to the part of you that _____**."**

"Hello and welcome. What may I call you?"

"What is your job?"

"Do you like it?"

"If you weren't doing this job what would you rather be doing?"

"Do you know the other sub personalities?"

"Are you working with them for the good of _____**?"**

"How can you work better together?"

You can then call forth another sub-self and they can have a conversation for the highest good. Have them understand each other. Then give any disruptive part a new job or have them go on a well-deserved vacation.

End by integrating the selves to work together for your highest good; **"All-for-one and each is you. No one actor is the star in the grand theater of YOU. You are a working cast, a team, a crew and together you make a perfect YOU."**

© Shelley Stockwell-Nicholas, PhD (310) 541-4844
Shelleynicholas@cox.net   www.hypnosisfederation.com

DR RICHARD NEVES' PARTS THERAPY

Two sub-personality interventions; "Parts Squash Integration" and "the Six Step Reframe" relate to each other. With them you take charge of parts of your subconscious mind and seemingly automatic actions like your breathing. When you think about breathing, you take control of it. You can hold your breath or breathe fast or slow. When not thinking about breathing, your inner mind controls it. Otherwise, you'd always have to think about breathing and could never sleep.

Parts therapy lets you consciously access, communicate and take charge of all parts of your mind including your subconscious. Parts Therapy assumes that you have all necessary resources to solve an issue and that all parts of you have one common goal: your survival.

DR NEVES' PARTS SQUASH INTEGRATION TECHNIQUE

When someone says, "I want to _____ but something stops me," opposing attitudes may not agree and conflict is like stepping on the gas and the brakes at the same time. What do you do to get the best possible outcome? Parts Therapy! Here is how to do it:

1. Identify conflicting wish or desire as a "part."

2. Put one hand out; palm facing upwards and imagine one part standing on that hand. Now, put out the other hand and imagine the conflicting part standing on that hand.

3. Have each part observe the other and describe what it notices.

4. Presume that each part has a positive intention. Ask, **"What is your purpose and what will that get you?"** This moves the client to the highest intention of the parts. Continue until both discover the same highest intention.

5. Have each part describe the strongest resources of the other.

6. Have the parts integrate into a new, powerful part with all the resources of the previously parts. **"Watch and listen to both valuable parts and allow your two hands to come together only as fast as those two parts can blend and integrate in the most comfortable and useful ways... so that both benefit. Each gains from the other to do great work for you. As you breathe, it's wonderful to know that your parts are there for you."**

7. **"Now think of the specific times and places where you want these integrated qualities and capacities to be help in the future..."**

NEURO-LINGUISTIC-PSYCHOLOGY

© Shelley Stockwell-Nicholas, PhD (310) 541-4844
Shelleynicholas@cox.net   www.hypnosisfederation.com

WIN EXERCISE: DR SHELLEY'S SQUASH TECHNIQUE SCRIPT

(Excerpted from her book "Stockwell's Hypnosis Dictionary Script Book" available on e-books and at www.hypnosisfederation.com)

"**Put your hands out in front of you, palms facing upward. Choose one hand to represent the part of you that holds the attitude of _____** (State the attitude of the positive result you want). **Which hand is it? Very good.**

Now, in your mind's eye, imagine this point of view, there on your hand, looking the way it looks, sounding the way it sounds, feeling the way it feels, smelling, tasting being this attitude and viewpoint.

What is its point of view? What would it like to say to you? Just report what comes to mind and don't concern yourself if it makes sense or not. (Pause)

What gift does this viewpoint bring?

What is its positive value? (Active listen their responses and dialogue until you feel they have said what needs to be said).

Good. Now, if there are any emotions or ideas that you need to let go of, do it. Good." "Turn your attention to your other hand and place your other point of view (or the part that doesn't want to change) **there. Let it look the way it looks, sound the way it speaks, feel the way it feels, smell, taste, intuit and be this attitude and viewpoint. What would it like to communicate to you? Report what comes to mind and don't concern yourself if it makes sense or not.** (Pause.)

What gift does this viewpoint bring you? How does it benefit you? (Active listen their responses.) **If there are any thoughts or ideas that you need to let go of now, do it. Good. Look straight ahead so that you can easily see both hands stretched there before you. Good. And let your two palms face each other. I am speaking to each hand, do you understand what the other hand had to say.** (Pause for a response.) **Each is starting to understand each other better. Now, one at a time, let each tell us what they notice and appreciate about the other. Or, what gift their job brings that could offer a positive solution.** (Pause.)"

You've listened well to both parts of you so it's time to integrate. Watch, listen, feel, smell, taste, and intuit them as they come together and blend what is useful and important to both parts, so they learn from each other. They now work as a team. Take a moment and enjoy this new more productive attitude.

Imagine yourself sometime in the future in a situation where these new positive qualities will assist you to feel great. Excellent."

© Shelley Stockwell-Nicholas, PhD (310) 541-4844
Shelleynicholas@cox.net   www.hypnosisfederation.com

DR. RICHARD NEVES' SIX-STEP REFRAME

Dr. Richard Neves parts therapy technique stops limiting behavior.

First identify the limiting thought or behavior and then…

Step 1. **YES AND NO SIGNALS. "Go inside and ask, 'will the part responsible for the behavior communicate with my conscious mind? You may get a picture, a feeling, or hear a voice. What did you get.'"** (When you get a response thank that part for coming)

Step 2. **INTENTION OF BEHAVIOR; "Ask the part, what is the intent of the behavior? What have you been trying to do for me by _____** (the unwanted behavior)?"

(If the answer is negative, keep questioning until you get a positive outcome. Example: If the disruptive part says, "I want to kill the person [your client]," ask, "Why do you want to kill them?" "To protect them from being killed." "Oh, so your intention is to protect them!") **"Communicate this positive intention directly to the creative part of you so that your new behaviors will immediately and permanently satisfy your intent to _____** (original intent of the unwanted behavior in this case protect you.)

Step 3: **THREE BETTER WAYS; "Have these two parts work together and generate 3 new behaviors that are more effective than the original behavior. Tell me each new behavior as you think of it."** (You may suggest some new behaviors to them, however, wait until you're sure that they cannot come up with more behaviors. Don't evaluate behaviors, the parts will tell you if they're appropriate.)

Step 4: **RESPONSIBILITY; "Ask this part to take responsibility for the new behaviors… Are you willing to use these alternatives, in the appropriate context, to discover how well they work?"** (Negotiate until agreement.)

Step 5: **FUTURE PACE; "Imagine, later today, generating one new behavior, in the appropriate context and nod your head… Good. Now take yourself one day into the future and again generate these new behaviors. When it's so, nod your head… Good. Now further into the future.** (4 or 5 weeks from now… 6 months from now… the rest of your life…) **Forever and always, you generate positive behaviors and intention. It so it is."**

Step 6: **ECOLOGY CHECK; "Ask yourself internally, 'Is there any part that objects to these new behaviors?'"** (If "no," you're done. If "yes," take any limiting part through the process again.)

© Shelley Stockwell-Nicholas, PhD (310) 541-4844
Shelleynicholas@cox.net   www.hypnosisfederation.com

HOW TO CHANGE A SUBMODALITY or MIND STATE FOR GOOD:

POSITIVE STATE: "Close your eyes. Think of a time when you felt terrific and everything was just fine."

SEPARATOR STATE: "Open your eyes."

NEGATIVE STATE: "Close your eyes. Think of the thing you want to release."

MAP ACROSS: "Compare the two things and now shift let the time you felt terrific engulf and take over the thing you're releasing."

LOCK IT IN and FUTURE PACE: "Open eyes. "Now you know that from this moment and in the future you are whole and holy and all is well in your world."

LOOK WHO'S TALKING
By SHELLEY STOCKWELL-NICHOLAS, PhD
"Talking to yourself is 'coo-coo,'" said the voice in my head.
It indicates disorders…(Or, was that something I read?)
Inner speak speculates. Inner speak initiate.
Inner speak sings songs that inner voices sing along.
The me I am is in-formation sharing internal inspiration.
"Hello" I say "How am I today?"
The answer's loud and clear;
"I'm happy as can be with voices that I hear."

NLP GIVES SUB-PERSONALITIES A HAND

1. **INDENTIFY.** Locate the parts of you that are in conflict; the ones involved in an unwanted behavior (like smoking). Locate other parts that have your highest good in mind. Put out your hand and place into one hand the negative parts and in your other hand the positive voices.

2. **NOTICE.** Close your eyes and identify each part with a visual, feeling and sound image… describe each carefully to yourself. As you do, your hand will take on the weight of each personality grouping and will respond to the weight. That way, you feel the balance or imbalance of your opposing viewpoints.

3. **CONVERSE.** When both sides have said everything they have to say about the situation, take a deep breath and let them discover any points they agree upon.

4. **MERGE.** When ready, bring your hands up until they touch and merge both attitudes. Congratulations, you have resolved your conflict.

© Shelley Stockwell-Nicholas, PhD (310) 541-4844
Shelleynicholas@cox.net   www.hypnosisfederation.com

EDIT THE EDITOR

"If someone with multiple personalities threatens to kill themselves, is it considered a hostage situation?"

LIMITING QUIZ

Do you live with your worst enemy?

Are you very hard on you?

Do you blame yourself for failing to be perfect?

Do you call yourself names like "moron," "idiot," "pig," or "stupid"?

Is there a part of you that goes haywire and out of control?

A limiting sub-personality says things like,

"I'm going to keep you sick and debilitated."

"You don't deserve any better."

"You'll fail."

"This is silly."

"What will other people think?"

"You're worthless."

"How dumb can you be?"

"You can't do anything right."

If these seem familiar… then who is this untamed critic, or limiting voice within? I call them "the Editor." To protect you, this sub-self can get cocky and out of hand and lend a hand to slap you down. This often "critical parent" can be more negative than your actual parents ever were. They take as much power as you give them and overtake thought and behavior. The Editor, if given too much power, inner-fears with your happiness.

DO THIS! AND ELIMINATE LIMITS

1. Imagine Mr./Ms. Editor in a physical form. Describe them: What clothes do they wear? How do they smell? What kind of vibes do they give off? How are they built? What kind of a voice do they have? Do they sound like someone you've met before? What do they do for fun? When did they come into your life? Exactly what is their job?

2. **"Thank you for your diligence. As part of our team you need to join the other sub-selves in a common goal or retire."** (You may invite them to wait outside the door while your other sub-personalities work toward their common goal. If the sub agrees to cooperate they may return.) **When all the "YOUs" work together, we accentuate the positive, eliminate the negative and don't mess with Mr. In-Between; We take charge of thoughts, actions and reactions and THRIVE.**

© Shelley Stockwell-Nicholas, PhD (310) 541-4844
Shelleynicholas@cox.net   www.hypnosisfederation.com

REAL LIFE HYPNO-REPORT: WES ROCKI, MD

"In a scientific study, a woman with a 'split personality' actually had different blood sugar readings depending on which 'sub-self' was present. She was diabetic in one personality and not in the other! Hypnosis successfully invited the limiting sub-personality to permanently "step aside" and her blood sugar levels dramatically improved."

© Shelley Stockwell-Nicholas, PhD (310) 541-4844
Shelleynicholas@cox.net   www.hypnosisfederation.com

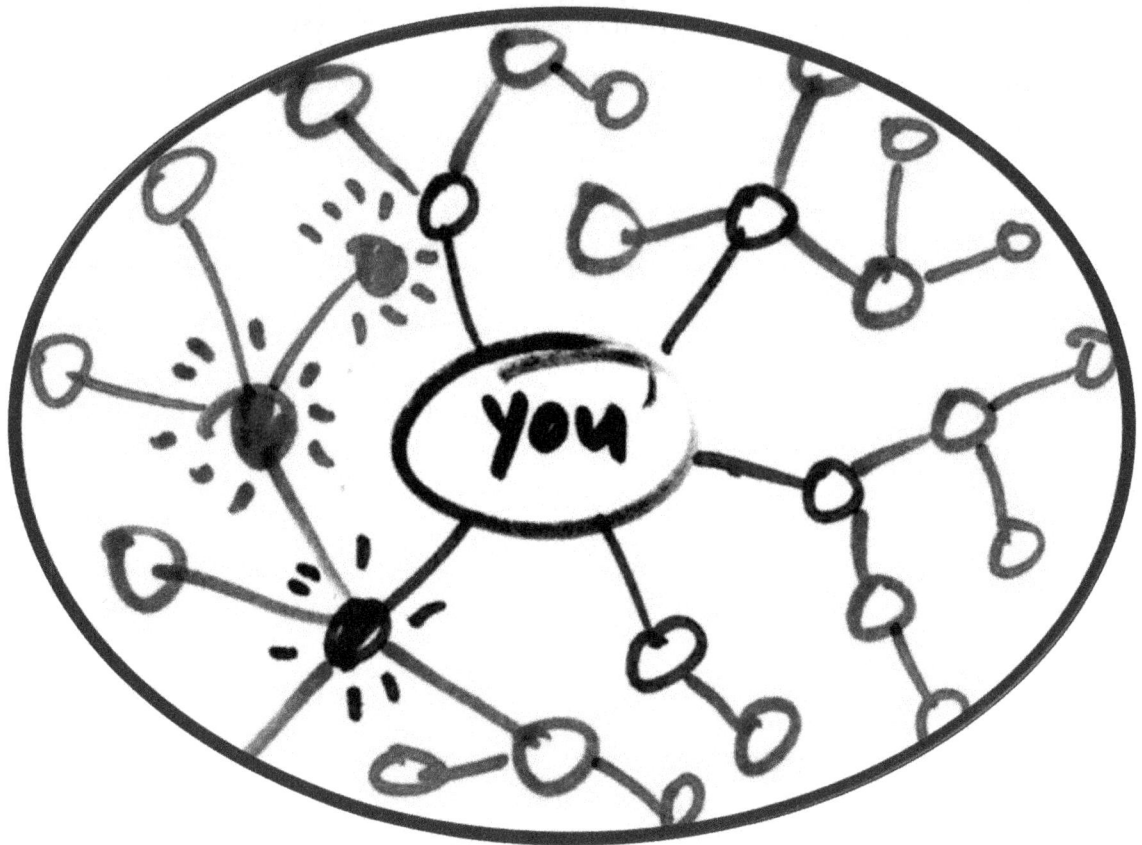

"The first thing a computer, designed to be like a human said was, 'That reminds me of a story.'"
    –Gregory Bateson

"The most powerful person in the world is the storyteller. They set the vision, value, and agenda for an entire generation to come."
    –Steve Jobs

© Shelley Stockwell-Nicholas, PhD (310) 541-4844
Shelleynicholas@cox.net   www.hypnosisfederation.com

TEACHING TALES & METAPHORS

Everyone loves "once upon a time" and metaphors. Storytelling takes your creative imagination on a magic carpet ride. Masterfully told tales evoke a listening trance as you step into a WINNING attitude.

Fess up! You love stories. After all, you constantly talk to yourself and make them up. Think of a story you say inside your head about an experience or a person…

Go ahead…Live it up… Think of a story

What's your point?…

How does that point reflect how you operate?…

If you like the story. Fine.

If not, do what my friend, Suzy Prudden says; "to change your life, change your story."

Pay attention to the messages you give…

Story telling, like joke telling, takes you to a punch line or ending.

Some tales you tell yourself are true; some true fantasy.

Your entire life is, in essence, stories you tell yourself.

As you talk to yourself (who are you talking to anyway?) you delete or enhance your Reader's Digest condensed version with the spin you give it. With each telling, your story becomes more true… for you.

Self-talk is self-teaching, self-preaching and self-hypnosis.

You believe what you tell yourself. It has to be that way as your mind– even when most rational– thinks and learns by connecting the dots and piecing together snippets of perception called "my story."

THE TRUTH BE TOLD

Policeman at 2 am: *"Where are you going at this time of night?"*

Man: *"I am going to a lecture about alcohol abuse, its effect on the human body, as well as smoking and staying out late."*

Policeman: *"Who's giving such a lecture at this time of night?"*

Man: *"My wife."*

What you say becomes "reality" and self-perpetuating suggestions teach you learn to survive.

Teaching tales are written on ancient temple walls, told in nursery rhymes and fables (like Aesop's), bibles and books like "Alice In Wonderland," "The Little Prince," "The Wizard of Oz" "Siddhartha" and,

NEURO-LINGUISTIC-PSYCHOLOGY

© Shelley Stockwell-Nicholas, PhD (310) 541-4844
Shelleynicholas@cox.net   www.hypnosisfederation.com

my newest favorite, "The Knight In Rusty Armor." Movies like the "Truman Show" also weaves a thread that can help mend your life.

When you tell your client an open-ended story, they use their intuition and observation to imbue the tale with their own wisdom.

Ask your client to "Create a story with the first thing that comes into your mind" and then, after they're complete ask, "If this story was about you and your situation what could you learn from it?" If they say "I don't know" suggest "Fine then, ust make up a story about what the story means."

STREAM OF CONSCIOUSNESS. You organize ongoing experience into narratives. That's how your brain stores and retrieves data. Your most enthralling stories invite the inner you to connect-the-dots and imagine and re-imagine what you think. Random bits are strung together into a logical sequence so it makes sense.

Events and impressions are grouped in meaningful relationships. "A leaf falls from a tree;" is a bare fact that causes you to search your mind for meaning. Symbols, archetypes, generalizations and pre-suppositions make up that inner story… "A leaf falls from a tree… hummm… must be autumn… like my grandma Ruth's tree that I climbed… when I did the leaves fell…" You and your associations, go off into the vast wide blue yonder of your inner library. Then something within you puts these inner references into sequential order. Simple words are cross-reference in an ordered cause/effect stream of consciousness. "A leaf falls and is disconnected from the tree. The leaf is dead…disintegrated to mulch-nourishing the soil for new growth" a story born afresh.

"A fox crosses a road."

"A person smiles."

"An ocean wave deposits a moonstone on the beach."

You connect ideas. You write the story.

GO IN AND FIND OUT. When attentive, you heed the tales you tell and take on to real-eyes is how YOU shape your perception. Keen perception overrides a bumpy ride on detaching trains of thought into another's reality tunnel. On the other hand, the diversion can open your mind to new possibilities. Tale-teller presuppose that their train of thought is a strong engine that drives home their idea. If you get aboard, you register clearly what track you're on. Are you the hero/shero or victim?

© Shelley Stockwell-Nicholas, PhD (310) 541-4844
Shelleynicholas@cox.net   www.hypnosisfederation.com

It's your choice when your perceptive eyes pop open in profound awareness.

I TOLD YOU SO!

"I was a know-it-all. Then I went to a hypnotist and now I'm perfect."

A great story someone tells you has you "drop the storyline" and go in to find out. You escape the outside world and enter the inside world of your imagination to– Spencer Humm's words– "discover your possibili-babies."

You often believe stories you hear… particularly if they came from your mother. You're naturally fascinated by mom. A good idea, because if you didn't get on board with her, you didn't get the milk and died. So you listen, learn and are captivated by the big lady… often for life!

A tale well told brings movement, color, value, and a web of understanding. Richly-woven tales are a welcoming fire dancing with flames of freedom and epiphanies! Retelling a familiar tale (to yourself or another) stimulates your sense of home.

ACTION!

Actions speak loudly.

Epic tales use studied rhythms, gestures, facial expressions and body movement. Hula, Tahitian, Legong, ballet, tap, puppets, and body language speak with words unspoken. Salome and her veils teach a thing or two.

Colorful words, surprising events, and bold images hypnotize you to listen. When well done, an en-tranced you comes to the dance. You enter the movie. You imprint a message. You're enchanted and encode and decipher words using your information and experience.

TRUE LIFE STORY

A fellow Toastmaster bored us with stories of why we should adopt the metric system THEN he did something amazing; he gave a speech about the "Sex life of the Metric System" and he finally got his point across. A good story that titillates, captivates.

PAY ATTENTION TO STORIES YOU TELL!

"The four grave diggers who carried a coffin walked around for hours… they lost the plot!"

Always tell a story with a message appropriate to the situation.

Listen, listen, listen to the tales you tell. They are a mirror that reflects how you think and operate. What does that story really mean? What spin did you put on it? Does the story build you up or not?

© Shelley Stockwell-Nicholas, PhD (310) 541-4844
Shelleynicholas@cox.net   www.hypnosisfederation.com

WHAT SAY YOU?
By SHELLEY STOCKWELL-NICHOLAS, PhD
Fairy tales bring cultural dilemmas; Macabre, gruesome and Grimm:
Of poverty, abandonment and often killing to win.
Cinderella, enslaved by ugliness, finds a man to free her;
And little girls everywhere dream someday to be her.
Jack with his Bean Stalk's a felon; a home invasion creep,
Who robs and murders his victim and takes the man's things for keeps.
Little Red Riding Hood's misled by a predator wolf in grandma's bed
Little pigs get eaten; Little children beaten,
Snow White's lungs and liver are ordered by the queen for dinner
Though cartoonized and imbedded with laughter watch what you equate with happily ever after.

Nursery rhymes, movies, folk tales, bible stories, old wives tales, poetry, parables, songs and dances stoke memory engage your imagination and hypnotizes you. You learn from example. What happens to a character, happens to you. Hopefully, "you don't have to fall off the roof to learn the ground is hard."

What message does the Wizard of Oz impart?... " An orphan girl whose house is destroyed, and a mean woman is killed, chases her run-away-dog into a surreal and upsetting landscape and is taunted with the threat of kill or be killed. She teams up with three complete strangers who seek help... from wizard who insists he will only help if they kill the dead lady again... Then he reneges on the bargain and leaves them to their own devices..." What is this story telling or selling?

SENECA STORY OF THE STORYTELLER

Stone speaks: *"Listen well. My brothers and sisters and I were created first here. We've been here since the beginning. We know everything about Mother Earth. Our stories must be kept and handed down so all will know the wisdom, knowledge and insight to get through turmoil. So sit in silence. Let earth speak and you will know."*

Teaching tales install meaning... the meaning you give it. Even if the teller intends to teach you a specific lesson like "trust yourself" or "overcome monsters of adversity," it's still up to you to believe it. A good tale teller presupposes that if you get their point it will help you. So they calculate which analogy might drive home an idea so you take the steering

© Shelley Stockwell-Nicholas, PhD (310) 541-4844
Shelleynicholas@cox.net   www.hypnosisfederation.com

wheel and drive yourself to the promised land. With that in mind, here are some terrific teaching tales…

HOW TEACHING TALES WORK

Teaching tales intentionally talk to you where you live.

They allow you to shift perception and make sense of tales told. Then you talk to yourself in a Reader's Digest version of what you heard and put your own spin on the story. All your life you condense, delete or enhance what happens and your stories stick as the "the way it was/is" and "reality."

When a coach tells a teaching tale, they grease your mental runway for a happy landing on your imagination. Then you project yourself into the story.

You merge with your favorite archetype and character. Their traits become traits within you. You're on a learning adventure and you like it. That's why shaman, ministers, politicians, advertisers, authors, teachers, moviemakers and sacred texts use story-telling to get you on board with their ideas. It is also why you must carefully consider what you are receiving and what stories you project to others.

STYLES THAT MOVE ME

There are many styles of teaching tales. Whichever you choose make sure it has a rhyme or reason and talks to the person where they live.

A right story, at the right time, to the right person, becomes a diving board into an unlimited pool of inner resources to become a life tale. Or, put it another way, a good story is like a slingshot catapulting you toward the bulls-eye of truth.

You know it's a terrific story when you look back upon it as something that evoked a happy, successful now.

Good nourishing teaching tools answer;

1. Who am I?
2. How should I act or navigate?
3. What's the meaning of life?
4. What's the world like?
5. How can I be me?
6. What do I need to do to live happily ever after?

HISTORY ALL OVER AGAIN

The earliest European carved and painted cave paintings in France and Spain have been carbon dated back some 33,000 years. These visual

© Shelley Stockwell-Nicholas, PhD (310) 541-4844
Shelleynicholas@cox.net   www.hypnosisfederation.com

remnants capture someone else's vision for posterity. We look at these pictures and they are animated by our imagination. We fill in the story of what happened before and after.

A story reflecting history and heritage brings the past to the present. Hopefully we learn from others mistakes…Then we don't have to fall off the roof to discover that the ground is hard.

DO THIS!

TEACHING TALE EXERCISE: YOUR PARENTS' STORY

Family Stories bring you closer to your heritage.

Tell the story of how your parents met. If you are not sure make it up.

YOUR STORY ABOUT YOUR STORY

"Here's a true story I'm making up." -Shelley Stockwell-Nicholas, PhD

Heirloom family stories, folktales, fairy tales, nursery rhymes, myths, legends, fables, songs, wives tales, fortune telling, tarot cards, religious texts are often calculated to have you conform to a belief or behavior. Then the stories you tell yourself, mirror and reflect your attitude and behavior. The language you choose and the tale you tell, become you.

DO THIS! TEACHING TALE EXERCISE

Create a story that illustrates a learning moment or principle.

THE HYPNOSIS OF STORYTELLING

Stories hypnotize easily because your innate DNA naturally communicates through cues and language. Once upon a time… and even now… terrific teachers and coaches tell tales. You absorb and learn from tales of others and they learn from you. You tell them your story, as they go inside themselves to make sense of what you just said. That, in essence, teaches them to learn more about how they think and operate.

Tailored tales fit the situation that suits you and gets you to tell tales on yourself.

Think about running and you stimulate neurons associated with the physical act of running. Identify with a story, and you stimulate your neurology and memory. Dr Lewis Mehl-Madrona frames it this way; An idea appears from the void of great mystery. It strides the labyrinth of your inner EAR, vibrated tiny bones, and transformed itself to electromagnetic energy. Then boldly moves from sulcus, gyrus, medial prefrontal cortex, to your posterior cingulate gyrus as your precuneus creates the plot line…

© Shelley Stockwell-Nicholas, PhD (310) 541-4844
Shelleynicholas@cox.net   www.hypnosisfederation.com

WIN EXERCISE #1: A SUCCESS STORY

A potential employer will be spellbound with a good story of problem solving given in a job interview. It gets them on board with YOU and may get you on board with them.

If a stuck story is succulent, sexy and seductive, you embrace it and it becomes "real."

If a stuck story is a horrific fairy tale, you may embrace it too. It's up to you. What you tab as "real" becomes the words you live by.

Whatever story, your voice, tonality, phrasing and words influence your body, life and outcome. What you say to yourself and others can energize or destroy.

What stories do you tell yourself about success? If the story isn't working out, make up a new, better story and stick to it.

WIN EXERCISE #2: RENAME, REFRAME AND TAME

This is a terrific ice-breaker when working with more than one person:

1. Tell a partner or your coach the story of your morning.
2. Take a moment and think if you omitted anything or would like to add anything.
3. Now your partner tells your story back to you as if you are the super hero of the tale.

WIN EXERCISE #3: ENERGETICALLY CHANGING HISTORY

"If you want to change your life; change your story." –Suzy Prudden

To change the past, or to help a client change the past, just separate your story and your interpretation of what happened from the unlimited options of what went down. In other words, rethink possibilities.

Ask these questions:

1. What words do I choose to describe myself or my situation?
2. Phrase it more positively.
3. Tell the story of your life in three paragraphs.
4. Tell the same story in a boring way.
5. Tell the same story in a most excited way.
6. Now tell it in a most profound way.
7. Breathe in positive words and let your positive story become you.

MENTAL LOOPING CONFUSION KICKERS

"Ambition is like a frog sitting on a Venus Flytrap. The flytrap can bite and bite, but it won't bother the frog because it only has little tiny plant teeth. But other stuff, like ambition, could happen."

© Shelley Stockwell-Nicholas, PhD (310) 541-4844
Shelleynicholas@cox.net   www.hypnosisfederation.com

–Jack Handey

NESTED LOOPS OR NESTED STORYTELLING

In days of French heraldry, warriors painted a small shield on their larger shield. The illustration on a Morton's salt box of a girl holding a box on Morton's salt and on that box is the picture of the same girl holding a box of Morton's salt…

Robert Altman in his movies like "Crash" uses this contrived device when he brings up a character, then another, then another and, in the end, they all come together. My friend Pam says "Altman tells his stories on each fingertip and, in the end, brings them all together in the palm of his hand."

NLPers sometimes use a story-within-a-story contrivance to evoke a mental confusion trance. They start a story, drop it in the middle, tell another story, drop it and then tell yet another tale and then– in a grand finale– they finish each story with one BIG message.

Peter Blum writes; "A common technique nests a dream within a dream and imbeds a message to the listener. Here is a story about breathing well you might tell to someone with a lung condition; 'A young girl, bedridden because of a respiratory illness, had an amazing dream of being a great opera singer. As you probably know, opera singers have the most incredible lung capacity to be able to… more than yogis even, who breathe properly and can easily retain air long and well as they inhale long, and exhale fully. When they breathe in, they really breathe in well indeed…. So, as the young girl lay there dreaming about being that great opera singer she…' You then continue the story, adding vivid painted details like the name of the opera singer, where they were performing, what their story was, and what it unfolds to be. This fictitious singer imbeds an inner story to reveal the outer one 'I can breathe fully even with my lung condition.'"

NESTED LOOP INDUCTION SCRIPT

"While meditating in a deep pool of warm water, a wise person, hears a child ask, 'How do you become wise?' The meditator looks into the child's soul and pushes the child under the water. The child feels light-headed from lack of oxygen….

Which reminds me… My husband told me to go the store and I tried to remember what he wanted me to get but my mind went blank…

Oh, before I tell you what happened... I was in Tahiti resting on warm sand and my body was so relaxed... just like a loose rag doll... when I thought, 'I am so relaxed... can I go deeper?' Then an amazing thing happened...

Oh that reminds me, my friend asked, 'what's it like to experience profound hypnosis where your whole mind and body relaxes?' and I remember my mom saying SLEEP NOW in a strong voice. It's funny, when she did that, my mind and body went into profound relaxation. SLEEP NOW! Just like that I went deeper and deeper, the way my friend wanted to know about profound relaxation, I went deeper. In Tahiti, going deeper then I had in my entire life. It's great to let go...

So when I went to the store for my husband, and my mind went blank for a spell and when I returned I had actually bought what I needed...

So the wise meditator pulls the child up from the pool and the light-headed child smiles. They are relaxed and happy and the question they asked 'how do you become wise?' is answered. It's fabulous how sometimes confusion brings clarity when you put it all together."

STRAIGHT FORWARD TEACHING TALES

Q: "Why is a teaching tale like a pencil?"
A: "It is no good unless it has a point."

What follows are some direct and popular teaching tales. Read each one and think of how you will use them to motivate yourself and others. Let the meaning think/sink in:

STORY CREATION

A great story intermeshes emotion, vision and passion. It maximizes an emotional experience for the listener or reader. The plot grows from the characters and situations. A turning point brings a lesson or awakening.

To make your story terrific ask...

1. WHO AM I? Stories about you are most compelling. Let your story reflect the person's truth delivered in way that speaks to them where they live. A great story lets yo focus, think, rethink about what matters. It lets your mind meander to answer; who am I? It again and again sparks in the heart. (A heartfelt story touches our heart.) Tell the story that embrace who you/they are. Affirm; **"I give myself permission to encourage my creativity and tell my truth"**

© Shelley Stockwell-Nicholas, PhD (310) 541-4844
Shelleynicholas@cox.net   www.hypnosisfederation.com

2. TO WHOM AM I TALKING? The person who helps the audience the most is the most successful. Immerse yourself in the genre of your audience and always keep them in mind as you think, speak or write your story. Use their language and play to their dominant senses and experience. Don't be special, be similar to the audience. Lift them up. When you are speaking you become your process and not yourself. In other words; get over yourself.

3. WHAT MESSAGE DO I WANT TO DELIVER? What story do you tell and why? What is your intention, motivation or passion in telling this story? Why is it important? What angle are you taking? How do you want them to think or feel? (Do you want them to be happy? Take some action? Buy something? Make the world a better place? Shift an attitude?

Feel a feeling? Or Understand a concept?) When you decide exactly what you want to create you can write yourself a letter. Then read what you just wrote. Does it stir emotions? Would I give this presentation if I knew it was my last one ever?

4. STRUCTURE YOUR STORY. How much time do you have to tell your tale? Stay within your time limits. Who will be the hero? How do they feel or think? What helps them? What hinders them? What event lets us empathize with them? What new thing, idea (or opportunity) drives them forward? How do they adjust to this new perception? What is their happy ending?

5. HAVE FUN AND STAY PRESENT

WIN SCIENTIFIC STUDY

"Nothing happens next. So let's count to twelve and keep still..."-Peter Blum

Richard Petty of Ohio State University had high school students write what they liked or disliked about their bodies. Half were then told, "Contemplate your thoughts and then check them for grammar or spelling mistakes."

The other half were asked to, "Contemplate your thoughts and then throw the paper in a trash can." As expected, those who wrote positive thoughts had more positive attitudes toward their body. However, those who threw their thoughts away showed no difference in how they rated their body, regardless of whether they wrote positive or negative thoughts."

NEURO-LINGUISTIC-PSYCHOLOGY

© Shelley Stockwell-Nicholas, PhD (310) 541-4844
Shelleynicholas@cox.net   www.hypnosisfederation.com

THE STORY TELLER'S STORY:

One day a storyteller coach reminded Jim, "Think of storytelling as a feast where you are the cook, server and the ones who come to dine. Each morsel, from appetizer to main dish to dessert, bring delicious flavors to your tongue of awareness… some tangy, some meaty, some saucy, some sweety… Tale tellers nourish your needs by delivering delectable delicacies."

A STORY TELLERS EXERCISE

1. Tell a story about why you are interested in story telling.
2. Then tell a story about what you learned by reading your story.
3. What is your story about stories?

HUMOR-US TEACHING TALE

"Many think history is a dull subject. Dull? Is it "dull" that Jesse James once got bitten on the forehead by an ant, and at first it didn't seem like anything, but then, the bite got worse and worse. So he went to a doctor in town, and the secretary told him to wait. He sat down and waited, and waited, and waited, and waited, and then, finally, he got to see the doctor, and the doctor put some salve on it… Do you call that dull?"
–Jack Handey

"I dreamt I was giving a boring presentation and when I woke up I discovered I was…"

"You can't deny laughter. It plops down in your favorite chair and stays as long as it wants."
–Stephen King

"To me, boxing is like a ballet, except there's no music, no choreography, and the dancers hit each other." –Jack Handey

A TEACHING TALE ABOUT STAGE FRIGHT

A gladiator, thrown to a lion, whispered something in the lion's ear and the lion sat down.
"What did you say to the lion?"
"I told him that every one is required to give an after dinner speech."

© Shelley Stockwell-Nicholas, PhD (310) 541-4844
Shelleynicholas@cox.net   www.hypnosisfederation.com

TEACH YOURSELF A LESSON TALE

Young Man to older man on the train: *"What time is it?"*

Older Man: *"I won't tell you because if I do, you'd start a conversation. You'd ask me what my business is and I'd tell you. Then I'd have to ask you what your business is, even though I am not the least bit interested. Pretty soon we'd be chummy and when I get off at my stop, you'll get off too. My wife will be waiting for me in the car and I'll introduce you. She'll invite you to come over for dinner and you'll accept. You'll meet my lovely daughter and fall in love with her. You'll probably ask her to marry you and I don't want my daughter to marry a guy who doesn't own a watch."*

Young Man: *"So, what's your business?"*

WIN STORY QUERY: Life-Affirming Stories

"Here's a true story I'm making up." –Shelley Stockwell-Nicholas, PhD

WATSON'S WIN TEACHING TALE FOR COACHES

Michael Watson reminds us of the fine work we do: "A monastery in ancient Siam had a great plaster Buddha statue. It was believed to be placed there in the 13 century. In the 1950s a new road was to be built and the statue moved. While being lifted by a crane, the plaster cracked. A monk noticed a yellow glint and chiseled the material away. Beneath was a solid gold Buddha 15 feet tall and weighing five tons!

Centuries earlier, the statue was covered with plaster to avoid being plundered by the invading Burmese. The people you help are like that statue and you are like the monk who chips away to find their pure gold."

WIN TEACHING TALE FOR LEADERS
YOU ARE A BUS DRIVER (Thanks to Jim Collins for this one)

An organization is a bus and the leader is the bus driver. To resurrect a sinking Fannie Mae (in 1981 with mortgage loans were $56 billion underwater), CEO, David Maxwell, told each executive; "It's going to be a tough ride; a very demanding trip. There are only seats on the bus for A-level people willing to put out an A-plus effort. If you don't want to go, say so and get off the bus… no questions asked, no recriminations." 14 of the 26 executives got off the bus and were replaced.

When everyone was on board, Maxwell got in the driver's seat and drove the team to resurrect Fannie Mae from losing $1 million a day, to earning $4 million a day! Maxwell left the bus in 1991, and his team continued on the ride— and from 1984 to 1999 Fannie Mae generated stock returns nearly eight times (7.56) better than the general market.

To drive your bus, first align all your parts– your sub-personalities– so all agree to go where you want to go. Make sure that those who want to go where you want to go are on the bus… then get rolling.

NEURO-LINGUISTIC-PSYCHOLOGY

© Shelley Stockwell-Nicholas, PhD (310) 541-4844
Shelleynicholas@cox.net   www.hypnosisfederation.com

Carl Jung, Fritz & Laura Perls, Virginia Satir, Milton Erickson

© Shelley Stockwell-Nicholas, PhD (310) 541-4844
Shelleynicholas@cox.net   www.hypnosisfederation.com

NLP TAKEN FROM OTHERS

Neurolinguistics "appropriated" the work of many who went before. Here are examples along with helpful scripts:

BORROWING FROM FRITZ and LAURA PERLS

Grinder and Bandler borrowed heavily from Fritz and Laura Perls' Gestalt work. Gestalt, means creates a "meaningful organized whole." They also took their theories of sub-personality dialogue, sensory awareness (VAK), suggestive questioning, verbal and nonverbal messages and the focus upon what you do rather than why you do it.

> **GESTALT AFFIRMATION SCRIPT: "I am now aware of my gestures, breathing, emotion, voice and facial expressions... My immediate sensory awareness and involvement supports my creative adjustment to life... I notice what is there and what I imagine is there as I come to my senses in every way. I notice what I see, What I feel, and what I hear. I pay attention to what I remember, imagine, emote, and verbalize... Respons-ability is my ability to choose my own reactions."**

The "phobia cure" or "the movie rewind pattern" (that has you play a movie then rewind it) was originally created by Perls who wrote, "To diffuse an issue, imagine motions around you as if they occurred the other way around, as in a reverse-motion film, where a diver sails gracfully from the springoard into water and then with equal ease flies back up from the water to the springoard."

ROLE PLAYING

Gestalt techniques let you role play parts of yourself. It calls you to note your words and gestures as underscoring what's important in context with all parts of you. You then "chunk it up" to a bigger idea that gives meaning.

REAL LIFE GESTALT STORY; Dr Shelley

In the 1970s, while attending classes at Esalan Institute in the Big Sur, I learned the Perls power of body language, role playing and attention to words and actions. I was told, **"Sit in this chair and be one part of your conflict... Now, move to this chair and be the other part... Let them have a full conversation."** Finally, I was instructed **"Stand up between the two chairs and negotiate a settlement."** Viola; Integration!

NEURO-LINGUISTIC-PSYCHOLOGY

© Shelley Stockwell-Nicholas, PhD (310) 541-4844
Shelleynicholas@cox.net   www.hypnosisfederation.com

PATTERNS

What the Perls' called "experiments," NLPers renamed "patterns."

PATTERN INTERRUPTS

The NLP "Swish Pattern" derails and disrupts a limiting train of thought to put you on track for a better destination. In Perls' words, "A good gestalt shifts attention to what you are becoming." The process is simple. You imagine a cue or image that represents unwanted behavior, then you program thoughts to switch to a new cue of the desired outcome. This switch/swap is often coupled with the verbal command "SWISH."

NLP SWISH/SWAP SCRIPT #1: Photo Finish

(Visually dominant folks like this one!) **"Put our one hand. In your mind's eye, visualize or imagine a photo of you doing the thing you no longer want to do. Good... Put out your other hand and visualize and imagine a photo of you reacting and doing what you'd rather do. Good. Look at the first picture in your ____ hand.** (The one with the negative behavior) **and imagine it melting away until it disappears... Let me know when it is gone... Good... Look at the other picture in your ____ hand** (The one with the results you want.) **Imagine the photo getting so big with colors so radiant, that you step right into the picture and feel marvelous in every way. Let me know when it is so. Good...** (Repeat several times, each time faster and faster... Finally) **"Take a deep breath and relax, feeling terrific."**

NLP SWISH/SWAPT SCRIPT #2: Delete An Issue (Thanks to Wil Horton for his idea)

1. **IMAGINE AN ISSUE- "Witness- see, feel, hear, smell, taste and intuit- an issue you want resolved."**

2. **IMAGINE THE IDEAL YOU- "Imagine an I-deal YOU free of this issue. This YOU sees, feels, hears, tastes, smells, intuits and acts, way beyond this. This YOU is happy, whole and holy. Give this happy, peaceful YOU you a special icon labeled 'I'm in charge' and install it on your mental computer's screen of mind... Good."**

3. **CREATE AN "I'VE GOT IT HANDLED ICON "Now give the old issue an icon... Name it, 'I've got it handled icon'... Great!"**

4. **DELETE- "Drag 'I've got it handled icon' to the trash and hit the delete button... Bye Bye."**

5. **DOUBLE-CLICK- "Now double click the 'I'm in charge' icon and let this YOU fill the whole screen. The system is now corrected. The issue will not bother you further... It's done."**

© Shelley Stockwell-Nicholas, PhD (310) 541-4844
Shelleynicholas@cox.net   www.hypnosisfederation.com

BORROWING FROM VIRGINIA SATIR

"Every word, facial expression, gesture and action sends a message."
–Virginia Satir

The NLP Meta-Communication Model taken from Virginia Satir brings awareness to unconscious messages.

Satir posed suggestive questions like; "What would have to change for you to forgive yourself?" She noted "two dialogues of communication" one of words and one of emotion" and said, "Sharing feelings is the ultimate step toward re-solving any issue."

Her role-playing approach had the therapist present various viewpoints or categories of behavior (1.e. distractor, pleaser, blamer, computer) to a client to open up their ideas.

SATIR'S AFFIRMATION FOR SELF-EMPOWERMENT
"I am me!

In all the world, there is no one else exactly like me. Everything that comes out of me is authentically me because I alone chose it. I own everything about me; My body, my feelings, my mouth, my voice, my actions, toward others and toward myself.

I own my fantasies, my dreams, my hopes, my fears. I own all my triumphs and successes; all my failures and mistakes. Because I own all of Me, I now become intimately acquainted with me.

By so doing, I love myself and am friendly with all my parts.

There are aspects about myself that puzzle me and others– aspects I have yet to know– so because I am friendly and loving to myself, I hopefully, regularly and courageously seek understanding and solutions to the puzzle and discover more about me.

However I look and sound, whatever I say and do, and whatever I think and feel is authentically Me… If later some part of how I looked, sounded, thought and felt turns out to be unfitting, I discard it, invent something new to replace it, and keep the rest.

I see, hear, feel, think, say, and do things to be my best. I have the tools to survive, to be close to others, to be productive to make sense and order out of the world of people and things outside of me.

I own me, and therefore I can engineer me– I am me and I AM OKAY!"

© Shelley Stockwell-Nicholas, PhD (310) 541-4844
Shelleynicholas@cox.net   www.hypnosisfederation.com

BORROWING FROM KARL JUNG

"Who looks outside, dreams; Who looks inside, awakens…" –Karl Jung

Carl (Karl) Jung was a practicing hypnotist (along with Sigmund Freud; they parted ways and philosophies because Jung was more optimistic about possibilities.)

Jung defined four modes of unconscious awareness– Thinker, Feeler, Sensor and Intuitor– NLPers redubbed these "Meta Programs" (They also became the Myers Briggs personality profile types).

Jung said, "We each possess a collective unconscious mind that programs all human knowledge as well as a personal unconscious." The NLP catch phrase "perception is projection" came from Jung who went on to say "We tend to take our most unconscious material and project it onto people and events around us." In NLP terms, the "meta-program" of you is determined by your perceptions and, one particular awareness is most dominant most of the time.

BORROWING FROM MILTON ERICKSON

"Everyone is hypnotizable when you adapt techniques to them. Poor hypnotists are the only reason someone won't enter trance."
–Milton Erickson

NLP "borrowed" much from Milton Erickson; his indirect, long, woven, non sequitur small-talk, imbedded commands, pauses, symbols, manipulation, confusions, obfuscations, analogies, metaphor and allegories that he termed "unconscious learning." His strategies were renamed as Ericksonian Hypnosis and the "Milton Model."

Erickson enjoyed sometimes hypnotizing people without ever saying the word "hypnosis." His backdoor style suited him well. Unfortunately, "true-believer" Erickson knock-offs are often poorly suited to deliver his style. I was horrified at a Ericksonian Conference to hear the most convoluted, esoteric, cumbersome, slow, and self-aggrandizing backdoor demonstrations… perhaps you might…and then of course…it felt to me like…can you imagine…slow death...

Milton recommended three helpful ideas:

1. **INDIVIDUALIZE YOUR APPROACH.** Play to the unique aspects of each person. In his words; "Most life 'rules' are arbitrary beliefs, not facts… Each person has a potential for a revolutionary shift…and the solution for every issue that may or may not be your solution."

© Shelley Stockwell-Nicholas, PhD (310) 541-4844
Shelleynicholas@cox.net   www.hypnosisfederation.com

2. **VIEW SYMPTOMS AS SIGNALS FOR CHANGE.** In his words; "Patients are patients because they're out of touch with their unconscious mind… Maladies follow definite patterns and a disruption of the pattern– no matter how small a change– can be a most therapeutic measure… Hypnosis permits them to learn more about themselves and their unconscious."

3. **USE THEIR IDEAS AS A METAPHOR FOR EMOTION.** "A person who wanted to change the course of a river found that if he opposed the river by trying to block it, the river merely went over and around him. When he accepted the force of the river it diverted in a new direction the river cut a new channel."

MILTON'S PARADOX

Erickson sometimes employed Baudouin's "Law of Reverse Effect" that he ostensibly learned when his father was trying to get a stubborn calf into the barn by tugging its ears. The cow wouldn't budge until Milton tugged hard on the tail in the opposite direction and the mooing bolted forward into the barn.

Paradoxical thinking, Milton said, breaks limiting patterns and forces someone to detach, muse and exaggerate contrary action.

REAL LIFE ERICKSON STORY

A hopelessly obese woman reportedly told Erickson, "I have to lose 150 pounds." "I will help you only if you promise to do exactly as I say. Do I have your word?"

"Yes, Doctor, whatever you say." "Very good… Come back when you have gained another 35 pounds." The woman reportedly followed his directions and became so disgusted with eating that she easily lost all 185 pounds of girth and then some.

MILTON'S TEACHING TALE

Erickson was quite the storyteller. His stories evoked trance and imbedded a message. His true and fantastic stories "first modeled the person's world and then role-modeled their world." His teaching tales, influenced by Charles Baudouin's 1920's book, "Suggestion and Autosuggestion," called upon allegories similar to those used by tribal storytellers. He also enjoyed employing emotional confusion similar to the stories most politicians tell.

© Shelley Stockwell-Nicholas, PhD (310) 541-4844
Shelleynicholas@cox.net   www.hypnosisfederation.com

He begins with, **"That reminds of a client I had who..."** or **"one of my children...when they were little..."**

Here are three an (uncharacteristically) short example of an Ericksonian teaching tale:

1. ERICKSON'S "TALK WHEN YOU ARE READY" TALE

"A lot of people were worried because I was four years old and I didn't talk, and I had a sister two years younger then me who talked, and she is still talking but she hasn't said anything. And many people got distressed because I was a 4-year-old boy who couldn't talk. My mother said, comfortably, 'When the time arrives, than he will talk.'"

2. ERICKSON'S "IT'S ABOUT CHOICE" TALE

This story was used to teach surrendering to the energy and chemistry of a situation and the moment: "Someone said to me one day, 'Dr Erickson, you appear to plan complex and artful strategies' and I replied, 'I never plan.' The truth is I planned without planning. You can plan what you will do or what you won't do or you can plan to not plan."

3. ERICKSON'S "STOP ALCOHOL" TALE

"A cactus is a special plant that doesn't need to drink for very long periods of time as life goes on. The cactus easily controls its thirst and remains quite beautiful. How blessed it is when pure water comes from the heavens to truly nourish it to the core of its being. As you think about the cactus..."

ERICKSONIAN INDUCTIONS

Erickson's zen-like strategies induced trance. He sometimes silently pantomimed the stages of trance and the person followed suit. Or, he used permissive suggestions like: **"You might not notice your eyelids are getting heavy"** (instead of "your eyelids are getting heavy.")

He'd say, **"Imagine how you'd feel if you were relaxed."** (Instead of "relax"). To open the door to hypnosis, he created conflicting demands and mental confusion that made it impossible to choose. **"You may either raise a hand or move your 'yes' finger when all parts attain inner harmony or integration." And, "Perhaps your deeper mind knows more about this than your conscious mind and if your conscious mind knows more than your deeper mind does then you probably know more about it than you think you know."**

© Shelley Stockwell-Nicholas, PhD (310) 541-4844
Shelleynicholas@cox.net   www.hypnosisfederation.com

ERICKSON'S INDUCTION SCRIPT #1: FACT TO TRANCE

"You sit there in that chair and your arms are resting on the arms of the chair (fact) and your eyelids are getting heavy and you are feeling sleepy and now you can hardly keep your eyes open."

ERICKSON'S INDUCTION SCRIPT #2: MY FRIEND JOHN

His story telling proportedly gave "greater personal control, free will and responsibility." "My friend John is very good at hypnosis. He easily closed his eyes, his breathing slows down and he relaxes completely as if he was sinking comfortably into the chair…"

ERICKSON'S INDUCTION SCRIPT #3: THE OBVIOUS

"Notice three things you see. Good. Now pay careful attention to three things you hear. Good. Now three things you feel. Excellent. Now two things you see…two things you hear…two things you feel. Deeper and deeper as you put 100% of your attention on one thing you see… one thing you hear… one thing you feel. I wonder if you're wondering how deeply you relax with this heightened awareness and if your eyes will close now or with the next breaths you take."

ERICKSON'S INDUCTION SCRIPT #4: VEILED AND VERBAL

"Now you might be able to remember back to a time when you were more relaxed…or more comfortable… I really don't know. But somewhere in your background you've experienced relaxation and have experiences of comfort. If you consciously believe that you will go into trance, you can go into trance. I really don't know if you are certain how deeply you could go into a trance and if you really know how quickly you could go into trance. I know a person your age who was able to go into- back into- trance and remember back to a time when they felt perfect in every way. Somewhere in your background you have many experiences of relaxation and comfort."

ERICKSON'S INDUCTION SCRIPT #5: AWAKE COUNT SCRIPT

"Look at an imaginary spot on the ceiling over head. Stare at the spot not moving… perhaps not thinking for the moment now… as your eyes, I don't know, may want to close. That's the way_____ (their name)… Now perhaps counting one to five, as with each number I count perhaps, I don't know, you feel much more alert, awake and relaxed. Starting with number one, you might want to measure the CHANGE you have made from the time you were sitting in my reception area filling out the forms, and two how you would feel as now three- there might be a hint of a smile I see and you feel there upon your face (Your smile brings more energy to their joy) as the number four now - yes, there is a definite difference... and five eyes open, wide awake, one, two, three, four, five- wide awake. Now sit still for a few moments and tell me about what is on your mind."

ERICKSON'S INDUCTION SCRIPT #6: BY THE NUMBERS?

"Do what you need to do to be comfortable within yourself... Good... How much more relaxed you are as you do what you need to become more comfortable.

You train yourself to remember when you want to remember or forget what you choose to forget... In a moment, I'll ask you to think certain things and, as you do, you'll discover that your mind becomes clearer and sharper so you will think more quickly and easily... Then later, if I were to ask you to remember something that happened recently or long ago... it will easily come to you and you'll remember exactly what you need to remember...

As I talk, let your mind go any place it wants. As you do, your mind will go exactly to the right place. This will happen automatically, even if you're not sure why it's gone there...

Here's an interesting way to notice your memory. Add the numbers three and five to the number of words in the sentence I will say. This will help you store the sentence away or bring to mind any answer... If you choose... [Pause] Here is the sentence; 'It's fun... to count... words...' [Pause]

You might not immediately realize the meaning of the sentence, so I'll say it again... [Pause] 'It's fun... to count... words...' [Pause] As count the number of words in this sentence, add this to the number you're holding in your mind... You may or may not remember the number you were holding in your mind... and that actually doesn't matter... The point is that to remember any sentence, just choose any number lower than ten and add that to the number of words in the sentence... I'll say the sentence again... [Pause] 'It's fun... to count... words...' [Pause] ... and you can add the number of words in the sentence to the number you chose... Now another sentence for you to count... This sentence has a number in it... I don't know. of course. if the number I say will be the same as the number you have in your mind... or not... that's up to you. Also the number I will say in the sentence is not the number of words in the sentence... Alright, think of

© Shelley Stockwell-Nicholas, PhD (310) 541-4844
Shelleynicholas@cox.net   www.hypnosisfederation.com

the number you have in your mind and make sure to store it somewhere in your mind... Then count the number of words in this sentence... [Pause] ... 'The number ... of words... is not ... fifteen...' [Pause] ... If you like, add the number of words in that sentence to the number you already had in your mind... And, if the number you have in your mind is an odd number, you can add one to it to make it an even number... so you can easily divide it by two...

If you've added up your numbers correctly... you most likely have the number twelve in your mind... Yet if you have another number, that's absolutely fine... It means that you chose a different number somewhere along the line... So you can replace that number now with the number twelve... that is easily divided by two... Imagine that you have exactly six bricks laid out in a line on the floor in front of you... six bricks, end to end... How many bricks would you use if you built them up into a triangle with those six at the bottom and one at the top... You would have six at the bottom... then five... and the next line would be four... and you might be able to see that triangle beginning to form in your mind's eye– Whether those bricks are house bricks or some other sort of brick– perhaps made of wood– that's fine.

The next line of bricks will be three... then two... and one, on the very top, to complete the triangle of bricks with six at the bottom and just one at the top... You may have already worked out that the total number of bricks in the triangle is twenty-one... but, if you have another number in mind, that's fine too... because now, when you stop counting things, you allow your brain and thoughts to completely relax You've done everything you need to do to sharpen your thoughts... So, even if you were only listening yet couldn't be bothered to remember the numbers, your subconscious mind understands about remembering... and it's been thinking about when you yourself were three or five... perhaps younger than ten... or maybe being fifteen or perhaps becoming a grown up when you got to twenty one... your mind knows about being even and dividing by two... Let your thoughts drift back to those times when the numbers were how old you were and what was happening then... whether it was three or five, younger than ten... fifteen or twenty-one or perhaps twelve... your mind knows where to go to remember ages... or times... or places... Things that happened a moment ago or back to other time... other ages... and your mind takes you where you need to go to remember what you need to remember...

© Shelley Stockwell-Nicholas, PhD (310) 541-4844
Shelleynicholas@cox.net   www.hypnosisfederation.com

ERICKSON'S INDUCTION SCRIPT #7: AUTO HANDSHAKE

This induction is enhanced by physical and verbal mental confusion and distraction. Here is a classic: Greet your client with a smile and seat them in a reclining chair. Look directly in their eyes as you lift your right hand toward them as if offering a normal handshake (stay alert). As their hand comes up, form a cup with your thumb and first finger. Instead of meeting their right hand with yours, put your hand (in cup form) under their hand that is coming to shake. But then your hand goes back just a bit—don't pull it way back, just an inch. The other hand goes behind the wrist so that it goes up. Just gently cup it and move your hand up in front of their eyes and say, "Look!"

As you pass the hand in front of their eyes and say **"Look!"** (Point with your other hand toward their hand. NLPers call this "presenting a new program.") "_____ (their name), **look at my hand and nod when you notice the changing focus of your eyes, and as you notice it, see if you can take a deeper breath than the one you just had and as you notice the changing focus... that's right... you may let your eyes stay closed on the next... that's the way, I will let you know when you are ready to let your hand rest and go all the way down...listen, can you hear all the sounds, aren't they clearer...?"**

Continue deepening with hypnotic suggestions.

In another version, you begin with a regular handshake, then a gentle touch of the thumb and slowly withdraw the little finger and a light brushing of the person's hand with your middle finger. The person's attention goes to the thumb as you shift to the touch of the little finger and middle finger and then to the thumb again. You then suggest upward movement as you touch the underside of their wrist so gently that it is barely noticed. This is followed by a slight downward touch as you then subtly sever the connection and their hand will becomes rigid.

ERICKSON'S HYPNOTIC EYE FIXATION INDUCTION AND REGRESSION SCRIPT

"_____ (Say their name and smile) **let me show you my hypnotic chair. Would you like a blanket? You may remove your shoes if that would be more comfortable.** (Recline their chair).

"Now _____ (their name) **as you find the most comfortable position in this, more-comfortable chair, gaze a little bit towards this wall in front of you or if it feels more right to look at the ceiling and see where exactly (half a second pause) you can select a spot and once**

© Shelley Stockwell-Nicholas, PhD (310) 541-4844
Shelleynicholas@cox.net   www.hypnosisfederation.com

you have chosen a spot, no matter where, but make it constant…let me know, you can nod your had once you've found that spot that feels right…that's the way…Now, _____ (their name) you may keep looking at that spot, wondering around it but coming back to it with your eyes in a non-stressful, easy-going comfortable manner of…and yes, your eyes many blink a bit more frequently and your breathing might get deeper and you may find that your mouth is a little dry which might cause the urge to swallow. And that is fine and perfectly normal before we step into the first stage of hypnosis, but not yet…I will tell you when. And it is perfectly normal once you feel this fuzziness looking at that wall/ceiling, aiming your eyes at that chosen spot. And some people have told me in the past that this fuzziness caused that spot they have chosen to change color or shape or move around an inch or two. And when it comes to this point we usually close your eyes…that's the way."

(If the client doesn't close their eyes, keep affirming what they see or don't see. Note slowing of breath, blinking, dry mouth, yawning, moving to adjust their position, limpness or tingling of the legs or arms, tension in the shoulders. Refer to random thoughts that fly in and out… (these are called "reflection suggestions.")

If they still have their eyes open, continue and affirm it as if it was your intention, **"I'm glad you choose to be consistent and look at that spot; some are not as persistent as you…There is nothing you need to do now before we begin hypnosis to help you with _____ (their problem). It's comforting to know that all you actually need to do is to sit, breathe and let your mind wonder… Let's make this agreement…Once your conscious mind notices what I say… I will touch the palm of your hand with my finger like this…** (Gently and slowly touch the palm of their hand with your finger. When you move your hand say:)… **and release.**

Now _____ (say their name as you gently touch their palm with your finger), **let's take a trip in time to this very early morning** (stop touching) **before you've gotten out of bed, before you came here to take time to renew yourself…Was it a sunny morning or cloudy morning? No need to answer… just think about it… How your day started is one of how you started many days, and today, you made a brave decision to change what you do and made it all the way here, you may have had to walk or park your car or figure out how to get around the building to find my office and now** (Gently again touch their palm with your

© Shelley Stockwell-Nicholas, PhD (310) 541-4844
Shelleynicholas@cox.net   www.hypnosisfederation.com

finger) **Here you are, you seem so relaxed and comfortable... just nod your head if you feel comfortable, that's the way...it's a good feeling isn't it?"**

Remember to use whatever happens, e.g. "and you might hear the phone as it rings far away as a magic wake up call that take you deeper...and I always remind myself how wonderful it is to be able to hear a sound where we live.

Now, _____ (their name) **I will be quiet for a couple of minutes to allow your mind to find its own comfortable spot in your own mind to focus on and relax. I am still here, sitting on MY chair...**

(Wait 20 seconds and then speak. You say "couple of minutes" but wait only 20 seconds to further confuse their mind and distort a sense of time. It's a classic time distortion method in hypnotherapy, but do not use it more than once in a session and for sure not every consecutive session.)

Now I will stand up next to you (stand up and move to the side of the recliner or chair). **I am on your** (right or left) **side to make sure you** (gently touch their palm on the same hand as before) **remember** (stop touching their hand) **the sense of... and yes, this is the way..."**

"And now _____ (their name), **one last thing before we GO into hypnosis now, isn't that amusing that we can hold a pen in our hand it just SLEEP(s) away...**(touch his/her palm as you say "sleep", release in "away").

ERICKSON DEEPENING EYE FIXATION COUNT DOWN

"Look at an imaginary spot on the ceiling over head. Stare at the spot not moving... perhaps not thinking for the moment now... as your eyes, I don't know, may want to close. That's the way_____ (their name)...

It's easy. Now, I will count backward, from ten. Ten is a one with a zero right after it... and as I do, notice if you can imagine the numbers in your head.

(Lower and raise your voice tone as you count down. You may want to emphasize one number. Some like to skip a number to add a incompletion mental confusion aspect)

We start with ten... nine... eight... seven... six ...five... four... three... two... one ... and zero. Zero may be a number or it may not be a number...it may be all or nothing... forget about zero... or become all and nothing... better yet getting more comfortable... this is the way it is done... easily now..."

© Shelley Stockwell-Nicholas, PhD (310) 541-4844
Shelleynicholas@cox.net   www.hypnosisfederation.com

ERICKSON'S WHAT AMNESIA DOUBLETALK

If your client says: 'I don't remember almost anything you told me after I sat on the chair...' you smile mysteriously and say, "**No need to remember. What you know is in the past as you sit resting. You know you are here and will leave feeling and knowing that you are in charge of the full measure of ease in your life.**

© Shelley Stockwell-Nicholas, PhD (310) 541-4844
Shelleynicholas@cox.net   www.hypnosisfederation.com

YOUR NLP SPECIALTY CERTIFICATION

Having done the exercises in this book, you've learned core skills needed to for Dr Shelley's "NLP specialty certification course." Of course there are many more NLP techniques to know yet this is a strong foundation for you. NLP is a dynamic compilation of many varied hypnosis techniques. Your IHF specialty certification brings you credibility and practicing what you've learned here brings you confidence in your life and the life of those in your family, at work, and with those you help.

Courses in NLP vary in length, cost and format. This book gives you a devine foundation and chance to receive your "NLP Specialist" certification for only $150 (US) or $165 (elsewhere). Included in this tuition is your first year membership in the International Hypnosis Federation.

Shelley Stockwell-Nicholas

(310) 541-4844

Or email IHF@cox.net

(www.hypnosisfedertion.com)

P.S. FOR CONFIDENCE AS AN NLP PRACTIONER NOW; DO THIS!

1. "Think of any limiting belief. If you do, notice it through your senses; see, hear, feel, smell, taste or intuit it. Hold it in your hand. Give it a color."

2. "Now think of a belief you used to have but now it is no longer true. As you do, notice it through your senses; see, hear, feel, smell, taste or intuit it. Hold this in your other hand. Give it a color"

3. Here goes… Let the thing that you know is no longer true absorb the belief you want to eliminate. When completely absorbed yu are clear as a bell. You now embrace beliefs that serve you best.

Good Job! Enjoy your NLP techniques!